The Strength of Black America

The Role of **Black Women** in the End Times

REV. CARL L. BROWN

PRESS
ACW Press
Eugene, Oregon 97405

Except where otherwise indicated all Scripture quotations are taken from the King James Version of the Bible.

Verses marked NIV are taken from the Holy Bible, New International Version®. Copyright © 1973, 1978, 1984 by the International Bible Society. Used by permission of Zondervan Publishing House. The "NIV" and "New International Version" trademarks are registered in the United States Patent and Trademark Office by International Bible Society.

Verses marked TLB are taken from The Living Bible, Copyright © 1971 owned by assignment by Illinois Regional Bank N.A. (As trustee). Used by permission of Tyndale House Publishers, Inc., Wheaton, Illinois 60189. All rights reserved.

The Strength of Black America
Copyright ©2003 Carl Brown
All rights reserved

Cover Design by Alpha Advertising
Interior design by Pine Hill Graphics

Packaged by ACW Press
85334 Lorane Hwy.
Eugene, Oregon 97405
www.acwpress.com
The views expressed or implied in this work do not necessarily reflect those of ACW Press. Ultimate design, content, and editorial accuracy of this work is the responsibility of the author(s).

Publisher's Cataloging-in-Publication
(Provided by Quality Books, Inc.)

Brown, Carl L.
    The strength of Black America / by Carl L. Brown. --
1st. ed.
    p. cm.
    ISBN 1-892525-94-1

    1. African American women--Religious life.
2. African American women--Social conditions. 3. Affician
American women--Social life and customs. I. Title.

BR563.N4B76 2002   277.3'008996
                            QBI02-200738

Printed in the United States of America.

Table of Contents

Dedication

I wish to dedicate this book to my beautiful wife of twenty years, Sis. Theresa R. Brown, who through many years has undergone some very difficult times. Though it was not intended, she experienced being misunderstood, being neglected, and even being abused emotionally. She has witnessed a change take place in this evangelist through the revelation that Black women are indeed the Strength of Black America. I love you, Theresa, with all my heart and soul; may the Lord continue to bless our marriage relationship for many years to come should He tarry in His coming.

To my children: Miriam A. Brown, Lester L. Robertson, Amber M. Brown, Erica N. Robertson, and Kevin G. James.

To my mother, Mrs. Iola Mae Brown of Baton Rouge, Louisiana, whose family and friends all call Ma Dea, who has always been a positive influence in the lives of all seven of her children. She is a good example that should there be the absence of the male role model in the home, godly principles will keep the children. I will always love you, Ma Dea!

I wish to give full credit and dedication to the Lord Jesus Christ who saved me by His grace and forgives me of all my sins. Who filled me with His precious Holy Spirit and changed my heart then life and gave me a brand-new start. He gave me the inspiration to write. I am not a writer by training, or by knowledge, but one who has been inspired by His precious Holy Spirit. I've come to learn that if I give Him what little I have, He is able to do exceedingly, abundantly, above all I can ask, think, or do.

A Testimony of Matrimony

By Sis. Theresa R. Brown

After accepting the Lord and having been saved and Spirit-filled for a little over a year, I received a word from the Lord as I was in prayer In January 1982. The Lord told me that I would be married during that year and to begin to prepare for it. He told me that I would marry a man of God and that I would not have to work outside of my home but would be a homemaker and raise my children.

I told my parents and family what the Lord said to me. They reminded me that I was not dating anyone and asked how was this going to happen. They even ridiculed me about what I had heard from the Lord.

My husband had been single and a Christian for three years and faithful to witnessing, leading souls into the kingdom of God, teaching Bible studies, and helping to raise believers up in the faith. He was getting a little frustrated and second-guessing his call to the ministry. He spoke to the Lord one day in his youthful immaturity and presented the Lord with an ultimatum. He said to the Lord, "If you have called me to the ministry then ordain me, or I will stop teaching and preaching."

His heart was right, and he said it in the right spirit; he did not charge God. The only thing that was a little extraordinary was that he told the Lord that it had to be done by the next weekend—which was March 27-28, 1982.

We didn't know each other at that time and were attending different churches. However, both of us were invited to attend a special ordination service of mutual friends on March 28, 1982. The Lord spoke to me and told me that I would meet my husband that day! My husband had to cancel a prior commitment in order to attend this special service to witness his friends being licensed to the ministry.

My husband had worked and ministered with the pastor and elders of this church where the ordination services were held. My husband was not scheduled by the pastor to be licensed and ordained with the other elders and deacons. During the service, the pastor stopped as he felt the Lord leading him. He turned to my husband and asked, "Are you ready to do what God has called you to do?" My husband was stunned! This was what he had asked the Lord to do that weekend! He was ordained that day and the Lord confirmed his calling.

I needed a ride home from the service that day and a mutual friend of ours asked Carl to give me a ride. Carl's first response was to say that he did not want to be distracted from what was happening in his life that day and felt like this was an satanic attempt to distract him with the attention of a woman at the time of his ordination.

The friend did not tell me what was said, he just waited a few minutes before approaching Carl a second time. He said I was stranded and really needed a ride. Carl yielded and said that he would drop me off where I needed to go. (Later that young man told me that he felt lead of the Lord to do what he did. He could have found me another way home, but he felt the Lord put Carl on his heart.)

After arriving at my destination we talked for a few minutes. His car was blocking traffic in the parking lot so we had to rush but did exchange phone numbers. After a few days Carl phoned and we went for a walk while talking. He told me later that a strange urge came over him the very first time we got together to ask me to marry him but he resisted and fought the urge. He couldn't get away from this idea of asking me to marry him and eventually went to my mother after a few weeks and asked to marry me. On July 31, 1982 we were married. We just celebrated 20 years of marriage!

Carl and I would like you to know that we compliment one another so well in life. We could not see this in each other, but because the Lord put us together we are meeting one another's needs. Let the Lord help you select your partner for life. He knows what you need and whom He has for you! All you need to do is "trust in the Lord with all your heart, and lean not to your own understanding, and in all thy ways acknowledge and he shall direct thy path."

Introduction

This book deals with some racial issues in America from a totally different viewpoint from how it is commonly dealt with by those who speak out on racial issues and the media and television. It is a book that deals with factual events and course of actions in a way that will bring help and healing to many who have been adversely affected by racial issues. The intent is not to step back in time, but to press toward the mark for the high calling of God in Christ Jesus (Philippians 3:14).

Sometimes in the heart of a minister, God will give him or her a message to be ministered. However, there are times when the content of the message is not to be delivered immediately. This is called being "impregnated" with a message. It is possible, however, at times to be impregnated spiritually and carry messages for extended periods before the Lord will give the liberty to release them. This has happened to me on several occasions.

On one occasion in particular, the Lord gave me not only the message but also the place it was to be delivered. Although I had the message and the place, He did not reveal the time. When the time had come for the message to be delivered, it was during a very crucial point in a particular ministry. If I were to name the ministry, everyone would recognize it immediately. The timing was absolutely phenomenal; the message was in sequence with events occurring within the ministry at that time after I had been impregnated for two and a half years with the message.

This is what happened to this evangelist with "The Strength of Black America." For more than ten years, I have carried this message in my spirit. I have learned that God's timing is essential when a special or particular message should come forth. I have attempted to complete this book after having the message for only eighteen months, and several times since, but it was not in God's timing. There would have been elements to this book missing that were needed to bring the balance that is necessary. Had I published it when I had the opportunity, those elements would have been omitted all together.

I grew up as child and matured without a father in my life as a male role model. My mother raised me along with six other brothers and sisters by her self. There was much missing in my life by not having a father to influence me. I never knew how incomplete my life was without a father, until I came to the Lord and He filled all the voids in my life, including what I missed by not having a male role model. God ultimately revealed His Word to me, Psalms 27:10 "when my [father] and mother forsake me, then the Lord will take me up."

On the morning of June 1, 1992, at or around 5:30 in the morning, I sat at my desk in my study reading the Word of God, which is what I did almost daily. On that morning the Lord spoke to me and asked: "Do you remember the message I have given you regarding Black women?" I did not have all the details to the message then, but I had for the most part some understanding of what He was asking, and I answered, "Yes."

Immediately the Holy Spirit caught me away in the Spirit and began to reveal information about Black women in America. It came so clear so fast. I cannot explain how the Holy Spirit does what He does. He caused me to write statements that astounded me. At the same time He flooded my mind with insight and revelation about Black women in America, and the history of Black people as a whole in America. I better understand now how Old Testament prophets, and New Testament apostles penned the Word of God on scrolls. The following is what I believe the Holy Spirit inspired me to write.

"There is a power so strong among the Black people of this nation that it is the very source in which God will bring about to deliver Black people from despair and despondency.

"This source has been so abused and misunderstood, yet within itself lies the potential to regain dignity and self-pride.

"In order for God to do what He will began to do very shortly in America, He will have to awaken this sleeping giant....

"This message is the dawning of that awakening.

"We have been hearing for sometime now that God is going to bring the Black man to the forefront in these last days, and He

will. But this power that I refer to now is the very power that will springboard Black men into position. Ironically, this power has been neglected and abused by the very product it will produce, "the Black man himself."

"This unnoticed power source (to Black and White men) that God will use is the Black woman.... 'The Strength of Black America'!"

Before this experience with the Holy Spirit on that morning, I had only part of the overall message. I thought He wanted me to preach the fragment of the message I had somewhere. I thought He just wanted me to speak on Black women submitting to their husbands. I told my wife I did not want to preach that message. I said that based on how I felt most Black women view submission to their husbands. But after He revealed to my heart and mind the power there is for any woman to be in subjection to the Lord first, then to her husband, and for single women to be totally subjected to the Lord, I was only too happy to write and preach about it.

I believe most of the church has failed to preach, teach, and demonstrate the truth about what it means for women to be in subjection to their husbands, and how single women should live for the Lord. I believe this is why many women do not want anything to do with the word *submission*. Even the way I once believed was also wrong, which is why I did not want to preach the message in the first place when I thought that was what He wanted me to do.

But for the woman who is first of all submitted to God, then in subjection to her husband, and the single woman totally committed to the Lord in the proper perspective, both are imminently powerful women. It is my deepest desire to transfer the information that is in my spirit to you, the reader, in order that we might understand what the Lord wants of Black women in America, and consequently all women in America and around the world.

One

The Molding of the Young Black Girl's Mind

Children at very early ages, and in this case little girls, are very impressionable. What they learn during those tender years will be the foundation of their belief system about who they are, and perhaps what they may become. What is taught during those early years will have profound effects on them for life. All parents hope that they teach their children those things that will have positive effects in the lives of their children, because if the effect is negative, it could have an adverse effect on the child for life.

During my childhood and since I have matured, my father has never been a part of my life and has had no input or influence at all. In fact, I have never had the opportunity to meet my biological father. I found out later that this is somewhat emblematic in the Black community. For as long as I can remember, growing up in the Black community, I have always heard negative statements about Black men, statements that unveiled a wide range of actions on the part of Black men, all of which was negative.

I also remember actually hearing mothers instructing their young daughters: "I want you to get an education so you won't have to depend on a man to take care of you. I want you to be independent so you can take care of yourself, because ain't no no-good nigger gonna take care of you." These were actual words spoken to young women and little girls while they were very young in regards to Black men. On several occasions I have preached this message "The Strength of Black America" to different churches consisting of predominately Black congregations. After mentioning this statement, there would always be a nodding of the head in affirmation or an amen by women in the congregation, acknowledging that they have experienced being told that at some point. Then I would sometimes ask for a lifting of the hand so the congregation could see just how many women have been affected by what they were told. Usually there would be a majority of women present raising their hands in acknowledgment.

After hearing negative statements such as that, immediately the little girl's mind began to be shaped and molded into a mind frame of negativity by her mother. The mother meant well by trying to protect her daughter. These mothers had been instructed the same way by their moms, who had also been taught by her mother the same mind-set to protect their daughter from abuse from black men because of dependency. This has gone on for generations, and it still is going on today.

As little Black girls would play games in the yard and around the house, they would say, "Let's play house. I'll be the mommy, and you be the daddy." There would be an argument over who was going to be the mommy, because no one wanted to be the daddy. I believe it was because of the negative image portrayed of real fathers. Even when little boys would enter the game, they, too, did not want to be the dad. I know because I never wanted the role either. Yes, I, too, played the game of house while I was growing up. But I could never figure out why being a boy I did not want to be the daddy. Assuredly the negative mental images were transferred from the older women to the young girls, as well as to the young boys.

Those older women were concerned for the safety and well-being of their daughters, so they gave those statements and mental images to young girls. Concern, which resulted from the ill treatment that Black men inflicted upon women for a very long, long time. The majority of these men were not taught how to love their wives, or how to respect them, so they abused them. Very few men had good examples of what it was to be a man, a husband, or a father.

The abuse that was inflicted upon women affected childrearing practices. The best defense women knew to give to their daughters was a defense of independence. Through ignorance this defense was fortified, not knowing what that type of mind-set that type of training would ultimately instill in young women.

The lectures the older women gave young girls helped eventually to destroy marriages, and even today they still affect marriages. Their efforts to instill independence helped to destroy trust in the husband and wife marital relationship. Because these teachings have been so prevalent through the years, the effect is still obvious among Black women even today. Even in the case when there may be men who have been taught to love, honor, and cherish his wife. For the woman affected, it is extremely difficult for her to overcome what has been deeply rooted in her human spirit.

So it was in the case with my wife and me, we struggled with the mental effects of independence for many years. After coming to know the Lord Jesus as my personal Savior I set out to live this new life; and so did Theresa. When we first married we both had wrong expectations of what being saved and married meant. I thought for sure she would automatically know how to submit to her saved husband. She assumed that I would know how to love, cherish, adore, and serve her as a wife. Boy! Were we in for a rude awakening when we discovered that neither of us knew anything!

We would discuss the situation that brought much tension between us and come to agreements. The agreements were when I would try to love her as Christ loved the church, she would then submit to me as her husband. We later realized this was not so simple. It was because of what was deeply rooted in both of us, even when I managed to come close to meeting her expectations of treating her right. She had been told that she should never submit to any man, for any reason. When the time came for her to exercise her will to submit, we realized it was not going to happen until she surrendered herself fully to the Lord. And I could not fully love her and treat her right until I surrendered myself wholly unto the Lord.

The lectures of independence oppose the teachings of the Word of God. The Bible, in the book of Titus, teaches that the older women should teach the younger women to be obedient to their husbands. Of course in our enlightened age, we have deviated from the truth of God's Word and have gone on to establish what we believe to be truth. As a result, we have weakened ourselves as a people and ultimately as a nation. The Scripture says it this way in Titus 2:1,5: "But speak thou the things which become sound doctrine: That the aged men be sober, grave, temperate, sound in faith, in charity, in patience. The aged woman like wise, that they be in behavior as becometh holiness, not false accusers, not given to much wine, teachers of good things; *That they may teach the young women to be sober, to love their husbands, to love their children. To be discreet, chaste, keepers at home, good, obedient to their own husbands, that the word of God be not blasphemed"* (emphasis added).

As an example of deviating from God's truth, the prophet Jeremiah spoke to the people of Israel when they were departing from the truth of God's Word, to go about and establish what they thought to be truth. Jeremiah, speaking for God, said in Jeremiah 2:13: "For you have forsaken me, the fountain of living water, and hewed out for yourselves cisterns, broken cisterns which can hold no water." A cistern is a reservoir for holding liquids. A cistern that is broken is unable to keep liquid in it. Jeremiah was proclaiming that God was the Fountain of Living Water. As long as Israel would look to God's truth, they would draw from His cistern and would receive nourishment that produced life.

Jeremiah the prophet said Israel left the truth of God and had gone on to establish their own truth, which could not produce what they needed and wanted. This is what he means by "hewed out for themselves cisterns, broken cisterns which could hold no water." This means that what they were doing could not produce what they wanted and needed. It would only result in failure to that which they were trying to accomplish.

Any teachings, traditional beliefs, or self-help programs that contradict the Word of God are considered broken cisterns, even though the intentions may be sincere, noble, and good. A cistern, according to Webster's Dictionary, is "an artificial reservoir for storing liquids." Of course, the word *artificial* means, "humanly contrived on a natural model." In other words, it means that anything that is derived from human intelligence is artificial when it compares itself to God's truths. Whenever Theresa and I would get into debates over why we had problems about submission, she would always say, "If you loved me as Christ loved the church, then I could submit to you." The Word of God does not suggest to us that we make any agreements to conform to what He says. When He says for a man to love his wife as Christ loved the church, this is not a suggestive statement; this is how He says it is to be.

When He says for a wife to submit to her husband as unto the Lord, it is not conditional as to what the husband does or doesn't do. It is what He said in His Word for us to do because it is best for us, for our homes, for our children, and for our families. Theresa and I have come to learn that what God says to us about marriage, He says it to us as individuals first, desiring to do His will. And now, through many years of trying to accomplish God's will for our marriage relationship, we have come to realize that we both must submit first of all to God's will for us as individuals, then to each other in the fear of God. And, Oh! What a difference it makes.

I believe this is what is wrong with our nation today; we have tried to answer man's problems with human intelligence. Secular humanism is a prime example of man trying to help himself. Secular humanism simply means a worldly way of dealing with the problems of humanity. Rather than allowing God the right to direct the affairs of His creation, mankind; Secular humanism has replaced the foundation of Judeo-Christian concepts, which this great nation of America was founded upon.

I want to share with you an illustration I heard a preacher give one time. It describes the human being with a need to correct problems in their life. Almost everything we purchase, appliances, automobiles, stereos, computers, all these items and more when purchased, come with an owners manual. When any of these items malfunction, we can open the owner's manual and discover the cause of the problem and do what the manual suggests and get desired results.

It would be correct to suggest that human beings also come with a manual, the Bible. The Bible is God's [who created man] operations or owner's manual. When things began to go wrong, you can open the manual and discover the area of problem, take the instructions and apply them, and get desired results.

If you purchased a CD player and began to have problems with it, and took it to a place that manufactured microwave ovens, chances are it will not get repaired. Why? Because the manufacturer was not the microwave company. In the same way, when the human being finds himself in trouble, if he goes to anyone else to get results, it is exactly as Jeremiah said, going to broken cisterns. The human being must go back to the One who manufactured him, in this case created him. God is the Creator of human life; no one else is qualified to tamper with another's creation. So when we as human beings attempt to fix each other and say through education we can do it, or through a positive mental attitude we can overcome it, then we have what you call secular humanism, which is another broken cistern.

In light of this truth, our older women today are still teaching the young women the opposite of what God has said about marriage. Almost everything in society today reinforces the same wrong teachings as it relates to marriage. Commercials, situational comics, day and nighttime talk shows, and organizations for women are teaching society that women do not need men; they can accomplish what they want in life on their own. Even in some cases where women work and bring home more money than the man, they suggest their roles be reversed.

It proves that we are still trying to cure problems with human efforts. This has not worked in the past. It is not working today, and it will not work in the future. We must come back to the ultimate truth, the Word of God. We must begin to incorporate the Word of God in our efforts to build a strong life, marriage, and families. He is the Creator of life and the marriage institution; therefore He is that Fountain of Living Water, and we will be able to get what we need when we adhere to His instructions.

For anyone to succeed in life, they must have a good understanding of the knowledge of God. Years ago in this great nation of America, Blacks were forced into slavery. During those rough and bitter, years men and women had to work the fields and other jobs from sun up to sun down. They were not allowed the luxuries of getting an education; consequently they were not able to read or write. Receiving knowledge and instructions from God's Word was foreign. This is not to imply that Blacks had no knowledge of God, or did not love God because they did. Blacks have always been and still are today a very spiritual people. But, because of a lack of knowledge and education, Blacks could not read the Word of God, and hence live by God's instructions from the Bible. This ultimately produced a faulty spiritual foundation in the belief system of Blacks.

In those days it was against the law for Blacks to have access to any educational material, including the Bible. In order for the Black man to express his love for God, he had to do it in his own way of worshiping God. So rather than having a clear understanding of God's Word, the Black man went about to establish what he thought was best. These are some of the reasons why we had, and still have today, in many Black churches traditional teachings that are not founded in the Bible. These traditions were passed on from generation to generation. This is why for a long time, and still today, Black traditional preachers preach with more emotion and theatrics than with substance and the knowledge of God's Words. Our experiences in church were based on how we were made to feel, whether we had good church or not. We were not learning very much about the Word of God. We would come out of church and say, "Man we had some good church today," but when asked what did the preacher preach about, our statements were, "I don't know, but boy did he preach!"

The question that may exist in the mind of some people is "Wouldn't God accept the way man decides to worship Him if he is not knowledgeable of God's Word?" The answer is "no," God cannot accept any form of worship that does not come from a true knowledge of what God did by sending His only begotten Son to die for mankind. Remember in Genesis 4:3 when Cain's [Adam's firstborn son] sacrifice and worship were not accepted and his brother's Able was? Cain offered a sacrifice and worship that were not acceptable to God. It was good to offer a sacrifice and worship, but they had to be acceptable to God, or they would be rejected and Cain's was not accepted.

In Leviticus 10:1,2, Nadab and Abihu offered strange fire before the Lord. Nadab and Abihu were sons of Aaron, the priest of God for Israel. They were instructed as to how to offer up worship and sacrifices. God said in His Word where the fire that they were to offer should come from, and they took it upon themselves to get it from somewhere else. They died because of what they did. Anytime we go about to do what we think is best, and not do it according to the way

God's Word says it should be done, there will be no life flowing out of what we do. Proverbs 14:12 says, "There is a way which seemeth right unto a man, but the end thereof are the ways of death."

Another question that may be present in the minds of some is, "Well, isn't it good that they did try to serve God anyway?" Yes, it was a noble thing to do, but according to God's Word we must serve Him according to the way that He instructs. Someone may ask, "How can this be done if someone cannot read with comprehension?" The Bible teaches that the Word of God is forever in the conscience of man, meaning that man was born knowing in his heart what is right, and what is wrong. This can be applied in the sense of knowing what is sin, and what is not.

An example that best illustrates the point I'm attempting to make is what happened to the children of Israel, God's chosen people. Romans 10:1,2 says, "Brethren, my heart's desire and prayer to God for Israel is, that they might be saved. For I bear them record that they have a zeal of God, but not according to knowledge. For they being ignorant of God's righteousness, and going about to establish their own righteousness, have not submitted themselves unto the righteousness of God."

God promised that He would lead Israel to a place called the Promised Land, a land flowing with milk and honey. Israel was called the apple of God's eye, they were His chosen people, and the land was called Canaan. The trip from Egypt to Canaan should have taken less than thirty days to be accomplished. Instead, because Israel wanted to do things differently from the way God was leading Moses, it took them forty years to make it to Canaan. Those that God had originally made the promise to never made it to Canaan. Israel made it as a people, but those whom He made the promise to never saw the Promised Land, with the exception of Caleb and Joshua because they believed what God said and were obedient to His will.

Did God love Israel? Yes, He did! Did He want them to make it to the Promised Land? Yes, He did! Then why did they not make it in? It was because they did not do it God's way, They wanted it done their way. Even Moses himself did not make it into the Promised Land for the same reason. He took it upon himself to do something God did not tell him to do. In chapter 17 of the book of Exodus, it tells of Moses leading the children of Israel from the wilderness to a place called Rephidim. There was no water to drink, so the people of Israel complained to Moses that there was no water. Moses went to the Lord; in verses 5 and 6 it says, "and the Lord said unto to Moses, go on before the people, and take with thee of the elders of Israel; and thy rod, wherewith thou smotest the river, take in thine hand, and go."

"Behold, I will stand before thee there upon the rock in Horeb; and thou shalt smite the rock, and there shall come water out of it that the people may drink. And Moses did so in the sight of the elders." God instructed Moses to strike the rock, and he did. In the book of Numbers, chapter 20, the children of Israel came into the desert of Zin, and again there was no water for the congregation of Israelites. Moses and Aaron went before the Lord; here is what the Lord said to them in verses 7 through 12: "And the Lord spake unto Moses saying, take the rod, and gather thou the assembly together, thou, and Aaron thy brother, and [speak ye to the rock] before their eyes; and it shall give forth water out of the rock.

"So thou shalt give the congregation and their beast drink. And Moses took the rod from before the Lord, as he commanded him. And Moses and Aaron gathered the congregation together before the rock, and he said unto them, Hear now, ye rebels; must we fetch you water out of this rock? And Moses lifted up his hand, [and with his rod he smote the rock twice:] and the water came out abundantly, and the congregation drank, and their beast also. And the Lord spake unto Moses and Aaron, Because ye believed me not, to sanctify me in the eyes of the children of Israel, therefore ye shall not bring this congregation into the land which I have given them."

This was no small act of disobedience that Moses committed. Moses, because of his anger with the people struck the rock, instead of speaking to it as God said to do. The Lord instructed him to speak to the rock and it shall give forth water. But instead Moses took it upon himself to strike the rock twice. The reason this was no small act was because the rock in the wilderness represented Christ. In the book of 1 Corinthians 10:4, the apostle Paul said, "And they all drink the same spiritual drink: for they drank of that spiritual Rock that followed them: and that Rock was Christ." Striking the rock twice was the issue; it represented the number of times Christ was to be offered up to die. Jesus was to be offered only once as a sacrifice for sin.

So because Moses did what he chose to do rather than how God said to do it, it kept him from going into the Promised Land. So as a people we cannot expect God to accept our way of doing things simply because it looks right, sounds right, feels right, etc. We must do things according to the way God has said in His Word. God does it that way because He knows what is best, and He wants the best for His people. God knows the future, He knows what's around the corner.

However! Thank God there is an awakening taking place among young Black preachers today to the Word of God. Hallelujah! Blacks are now beginning to come out of traditional beliefs because of this wonderful awakening, glory to God. Black people have always loved God and tried to serve Him, but when they tried without truth as a foundation, they always were sidetracked, even though they loved Him. This is why the psalmist David wrote Psalms 119:105: "Thy Word is a lamp unto my feet, and a light unto my path." Again David said in Psalms 119:11:"Thy Word have I hid in my heart, that I might not sin against God."

So when the women of old taught young girls about being women, the teachings, however well meaning they were, were not exactly according to the Word of God. Second Timothy 3:16 says, "All scripture is given by inspiration of God, and is profitable for doctrine, for reproof, for correction and instruction in righteousness, that the man of God may be perfect throughly furnished unto all good works." It is important to point out that the word *man* in this scripture does not mean "male in gender," but "male and female" as created in the image of God.

So the teachings of God's Word are what cause man to become what God intended. The mothers of old molded the minds of young girls, based on the experiences they had with Black men. Also based on the knowledge of traditional teachings. They did not mold the minds of the young girls with the Word of God. Over the years, our women and children have suffered at the hands of Black men who knew nothing of how to love their wives and children as God intended. This was largely due to the fact that we did not have a foundation of God's Word in our churches or in our homes. Black men were never challenged to take their places in the home as God intended. Once again, I reiterate that older women taught the best they could to protect their daughters from the abuse of Black men. The problem with that was that the only defense was one of independence, which is totally different from what it takes for a home to survive and to be healthy and happy.

God has made provision for women who are married to men who do not treat their wives with respect and love. The reason men do not treat their wives right is because they do not have a personal relationship with the Lord. In a case like this, the woman has a powerful recourse she can adhere to. She can be obedient to the Word of God and use the power of her influence with God so the Holy Spirit can turn her husband around. God said she could do it! Women have just refused to allow themselves to be used by God to win their husbands over to the Lord by their obedience to God's Word.

Here is what the Word of God says in 1 Peter 3:1,6: "Likewise you wives, be in subjection to your own husbands; that, if any obey not the word, they also may without the word be won by the conversation of the wives; while they behold your chaste conversation coupled with fear. Whose adorning let it not be that outward adorning of plaiting the hair, and of wearing of gold, or putting on of apparel; but let it be the hidden man of the heart, in that which is not corruptible, even the ornament of a meek and quiet spirit, which is in the sight of God of great price. For after this manner in the old time the holy women also who trusted in God, adorned themselves, being in subjection unto their own husbands."

It is important to point out that the word *conversation* has a different meaning in the Greek as it is intended in this scripture to be used. The meaning of the word *conversation* in Greek means "conduct or life-style." So the way that a woman conducts herself, or what she portrays to her husband is what will win him over, not necessarily witnessing or preaching to him.

This is guaranteed to work according to God's Word, so if there is a woman out there who wants to see her husband saved, apply this truth and watch the Lord do what He said He would do. If God said it, He will do it. If He spoke it, He will bring it to pass. Numbers 23:19 says, "God is not a man, that he should lie; neither the son of man, that he should repent: hath he said, and shall he not do it? Or hath he spoken, and shall he not make it good?"

The Word of God as It Relates to Women, Young Women, Wives, and Widows

The Word of God has much to say about women in all aspects of life. Many preachers as well as well-meaning people have distorted what God's Word has to say about women. Some think that women should be second-class citizens, or subservient to men in society and treated with less respect. None of which is true; this is even reflected in the difference of pay and promotion in the work place. Jesus Christ liberated and respected women during His time on earth far more than society at that time. One such example can be found in the Scriptures; in the book of St. John, a man and a woman were caught in the act of adultery, so the scribes and Pharisee caught the woman and brought her before Jesus to be judged.

St. John 8:3,5 says, "And the scribes and Pharisees brought unto him a woman taken in adultery; and when they had set her in the midst, they say unto him, Master, this woman was taken in adultery, in the very act. Now Moses in the law commanded us, that such should be stoned: but what sayest thou?" What they were saying was true. They used the Law given to Moses to judge the woman. But they did not appropriate the Law correctly. Let's see exactly what Moses said regarding committing the act of adultery. Leviticus 20:10 says,

"And the man that committeth adultery with another man's wife, even he that committeth adultery with his neighbor's wife, the adulterer and the adulteress shall be put to death."

The Law said that both the man and the woman should be put to death. The scribes and Pharisees brought only the woman before Jesus to be judged according to the Law. It shows how women were treated with less respect and admirations than men were. Jesus did not judge the woman. He said to them, "Let he that is without sin among you cast the first stone." None of them could do it. They couldn't do it because their own conscious convicted them, and they could not condemn her. Jesus, in turn, said to the woman, "Neither do I condemn thee go and sin no more."

The apostle Paul wrote the books of First and Second Timothy to the young pastor, Timothy. Among many other things he addressed within the church, he dealt with women, young women, wives and widows at home and in the church. He starts by responding to the taking care of widows in the church. In 1 Timothy 5:3 he writes, "Honour widows that are widows indeed, but if any widow have children or nephews, let them learn first to show piety at home, and to requite their parents: for that is good and acceptable before God." Verse eight goes on to say, "But if any provide not for his own, and especially for those of his own house, he hath denied the faith, and is worst than an infidel."

The word *piety* used here means "to show faithfulness to something to which one is bound by pledge or duty." The word *requite* means "to make suitable return to for a benefit or service received." Paul was informing the church not to take on this responsibility of supporting a widow if she had family members who were failing to show piety. But he also instructed that if the woman was indeed a widow, with no help at home, then the church should support her. However, that support should come only when certain criteria are met.

Those criteria are as follows: she should trust in God, continue humbly making prayers before God night and day, she should be sixty years old or older, have a good report of good works, have raised her children properly, lodged strangers, taken care of other Christian brethren and sisters, etc. If the widow fits the criteria, then the church should support her. In some churches it is believed that if someone is a member and has some financial trouble, it is the church's responsibility to help them. While this very well may be a noble act, it is not scripture that the church should take on this burden. There is certainly nothing wrong with helping people in need, but it is not something that we can use as scripture foundations for the church to do. Can you imagine what would happen if everyone in the church experienced a problem financially and the church would help?

God intended for showing piety to take place in the life of all families of the world. Fathers and mothers should raise their children in the right way, meaning in the way God determined. When the children grow older, they should in turn take care of their parents, if the parents can no longer take care of themselves. However, today in America this is not happening as needed. Families are no longer functioning like a loving unit. When parents grow old, chances are they will be put into a nursing home. This happens for various reasons, some of which I will try to reveal. Parents may have to go to a nursing home if all of the children of those parents work and cannot give the necessary attention to the parents as needed.

Many parents have serious health problems and need medical attention that comes from a professional staff provided by nursing homes. Parents that did not raise their children properly are more likely to be put in nursing homes, even though none of the above issues exists. The children of parents such as this are not in close relationship to their fathers and mothers. This has happened far too often in the Black community. As children grow older, they tend to grow distant because of the lack of intimate relationship and unresolved issues with their parents while growing up.

Because of this there is no closeness in the parent-child relationship, so the child feels estranged and distant. I am sure there are many and varied reasons as to why this is the case.

In some cases children are made to feel by parents that they owe them for having given birth to them. What this amounts to is that when the child matures into adulthood, they do not have the loving respect for their parents as they should and perhaps would like to have. Many parents have made that mistake and wonder why their children are so distant when they really need and want them to be close.

I remember visiting nursing homes for the elderly and talking with older people, all of whom were Black. Most had the same story to tell: they were very lonely, and they were angry with their children because they did not come to see them often. I have met older people who would not see their children until Christmas and Thanksgiving each year, and sometimes not at all. I remember feeling terrible about this and asking God why such a thing happens? Then it came to me: most of the parents did not raise their children the way God intended. This is not an attempt to be mean spirited, because there are people right now who are hurting because of this. I just pray that someone will hear this and not let it happen to them. And just maybe one of those parents could be reading this book right now and need to know how to correct a wrong.

Many of these parents went to church almost every Sunday, and still their children are not close to them in relationship. Just going to church alone is not grounds enough to say that the children were properly raised the way God intended. There must the application of God's Word in the home. And there must be demonstration of the Christian life portrayed by the parents to the children. I heard a preacher somewhere say one time about being an example in a negative way. He said, "What you do speaks so loud, I cannot hear what you are saying." Many parents thought just saying the right thing was sufficient enough to train children in the right way.

On the other hand, when parents raise their children according to how God says they should be raised, then there will be such a closeness and respect. The Bible in Proverbs, says, "Train up a child in the way that he should go, when he is old he will not depart from it." This does not mean that when a child is trained properly according to God's Word, they will always do everything right. It does, however, mean that should a child go the wrong way in life, that the foundation of truth that was put in them would ultimately bring them back to the ways of his or her foundational teachings.

A child will grow up to appreciate parents who took the time to love them, talk to them, discipline them, demonstrate tough love, and spend time with them, etc. The type of piety that will be returned to the parents who did the right things will be that of a willingness to be obligated to the parent. It will not be a feeling of obligation from a sense of duty. The results will be a love, respect, and intimacy.

The apostle Paul addresses the issue of the married woman. What does God's Word say in regards to being a wife? Ephesians 5:22, 24 says, "Wives, submit yourselves unto your own husbands, as unto the Lord. For the husband is the head of the wife, even as Christ is the head of the church: and he is the savior of the body. Therefore as the church is subject unto Christ, so let the wives be to their own husbands in everything." In America today, this thought that was originated in the heart of God is detested among most Black women of this nation, as well as women of different ethnic origin.

But for most Black women, it has never really been a part of her thinking. The abuse that Black women were subjected to forced them to be independent in their thinking of their husbands. On the other hand, it was somewhat the opposite in the White community. This nation of America was founded on the Word of God. White men and women had good education even while America was in her infant stages. White churches were given sermons loaded with clear understanding of the Word of God as it relates to the marriage and the structure of the home. The husband and wife's responsibility to God and to each other were clearly understood.

The husband would work to support his family, while the wife also with a good education would train and educate the children at home. While being in subjection to her husband, their home was in divine order. Even if the home in itself was not Christian in nature, the principles were adapted. The children learned to respect authority because their mother demonstrated how to do it every day in the home. Through the years, there's been a breakdown in the family structure in the white homes, just as it has always been in Black homes. Black America is just now beginning to awaken to the truth of God's Word. For the last half a century, White men have begun falling away from the teachings handed down to them. White women have felt the need to start organizations to gain their independence, thus resulting in a breakdown in the family structure.

Why would God say that wives should submit to their husbands? To answer that question we must refer to what God himself said. I will use two scripture references to answer the question. In the book of Genesis, chapters 1 and 2, God created man in His own image. God instructed him not to eat from the tree of the knowledge of good and evil. After God created man, and named him Adam, He gave him specific instructions as to what to do and not to do. Then God said that it was not good that man be alone, so he put Adam to sleep and from his rib made a woman. God then used this term about the woman, whose name would be Eve. He said, "I will make a help meet for him." God did not say a "help mate." He used the term "help meet." Oftentimes this term is misunderstood by clergy and presented wrong to congregations. This term was used because Adam was the only human being created at the time: The word *meet* means "someone suitable for man to converse with." Since Adam could not communicate on an intellectual, emotional, or sexual dimension with the animals, he needed someone equal to him just as intellectual, emotional, sexual, wise, and able to reason.

The church has taught far too long that the woman was a help-mate. That she was to be some kind of servant for the man. To help him to succeed in life; this concept is not at all proper. Although many women are capable of helping men to succeed, and God knows we men need the help. The term "help meet" was used because Adam needed to have a companion suitable for him as a human being. Not that he could dominate her, or for her to be subservient to him. But that she would be his equal, his lover, and his companion to walk with in life.

Although this was true and the way God had intended, something had to happen to cause God to have one to rule over the other. After God told Adam about what tree he could not eat from, Adam obviously informed Eve of what God had said to him. That he was to eat from the tree of life and not from the tree of the knowledge of good and evil. We know that he told Eve this, because when she was tempted by the serpent to eat from the tree, she said that they should not eat from it. She had not yet been taken from Adam when God instructed him about the tree. After she bit from the fruit of the tree first in disobedience, she then took the fruit to Adam and he did eat as well.

I want to explain the whole event that occurred in the Garden of Eden so it will not be misunderstood. When God created Adam, he was created in the very image of God. Adam was created without sin, and he was to live forever without dying. There are two trees in the garden that are mentioned. One was the tree of Life, and the other was the tree of the knowledge of good and evil. God told Adam he was only to eat from the tree of life. This would allow him to continue to live forever. Then God commanded Adam he was not to eat from the tree of the knowledge of good and evil.

This was a very serious commandment of God, which carried grave consequences if not obeyed. God told Adam that the very day he would eat from that tree he would die. The word *die*, as it is used here, does not mean to cease to exist in this life, as we understand it. It meant that if he was to die as a result of eating from this tree, he was going to be separated from God's presence because the act of sin causes separation. This is why God did not want him to eat from this tree. That is exactly what happened they ate from the tree, and they were separated from the garden and from the presence of God.

After the act of disobedience was committed, God came and inquired as to why they did what they did. Because of what the woman "Eve" did, God said in Genesis 3:16, "I will greatly multiply thy sorrow and thy conception; in sorrow thou shalt bring forth children; and thy desire shall be to thy husband, and he [*shall rule over thee.*]"

Perhaps many would have a problem with God saying such a thing. But when you really understand what happened as a result of the act, then you might understand it better. Women are, in most cases, far more sensitive to things than men are. There is a tendency to lean more to their feelings and emotions. Satan, who used the serpent to deceive Eve, knew that if he would entice her to get her to reason with her emotions, then she might stumble, and indeed she did. Then the Lord spoke to Adam in Genesis 3:17: "And unto Adam he said, because thou hast hearkened unto the voice of thy wife, and hast eaten of the tree, of which I commanded thee saying, Thou shalt not eat of it: cursed is the ground for thy sake; in sorrow shalt thou eat of it all the days of thy life."

The apostle Paul referred to this situation when he was writing to Timothy a young pastor in the New Testament. In the book of 1 Timothy 2:13-14, Paul said, "For Adam was first formed, then Eve. And Adam was not deceived, but the woman being deceived was in transgression." And because of this transgression by the woman Eve, God said that her husband would rule over her.

The apostle Paul also addresses the subject of young women. What does God say about young women? Paul said in 1 Timothy 5:14-15: "I will therefore that the younger women marry, bear children, guide the house, give none occasion to the adversary to speak reproachfully. For some have already turned aside after Satan."

"I will therefore that the younger women marry." Paul was declaring that God's will is that young women marry. God is the Creator of the oldest institution known to mankind, the marriage relationship. There are several reasons why God wants men to marry women, and for women to marry men. (1) God said that it is not good that man be alone. (2) The marriage union typifies the union between Christ and His church. (3) When children are born to this marriage relationship, they will have both a mother and father to raise them in the nurture and admonition of the Lord.

Many young Black women and girls are having babies out of wedlock; some as young as twelve years old. The Bible teaches that participating in sexual relationships prior to marriage is wrong. I understand this may not be acceptable in society today, but it is still the will of God. Look at the results of sex before marriage, excluding the fact that venereal diseases and AIDS are at epidemic proportions. In some cases, we have eighteen-year-olds with three and four children and not married. I do not mean to be critical, but what does this do to a young woman who is not married and perhaps did not complete school? Younger women and girls may be physically capable and ready for a sexual relationship; but they are not ready for the emotional turbulence that comes along with it.

Not to mention what this does for the raising of the children. The cycle is started all over again with the children. God's will is for the young woman to marry, then bear children—in that order. To some few people God has given the ability to keep themselves sexually without marrying. This is what was done with the apostle Paul. Paul said in 1 Corinthians 7:7-8: "For I would that all men were even as I myself. But every man hath his proper gift of God. I say therefore to the unmarried and widows, it is good for them if they abide even as I. But if they cannot contain, let them marry."

"Bear Children." God is delighted when children are born. The Bible says that children are God's heritage. The heavenly Father loves all children, and God has a purpose for their life, whether they are born in marriage or out of wedlock. Obviously His will and preference is for children to be born to parents who are married to each other. Then the children can have a proper example of what marriage is with their own father and mother as parents in the same home. The parents should train the children in the way of the Lord, so that the children can have knowledge of God. On the contrary, what is happening today is just the opposite.

"Guide the house." When a young woman marries, God's will is for her to guide the house. What this means is that she should have some say-so in the decision-making in the home. Many men, Black men in particular, do not like to have their wives in on the decisions in the home. In most cases, it would be better for the home for the wife to handle the financial budget for the home. She knows what it takes to run a home. She's keen on many things that most men are absolutely ignorant of. Many men do not even allow their wives to handle the checkbook, grocery shop, or shop for the children without checking with him first. This is wrong.

As for my house, Theresa handles all of the finances, the budget, the checkbook, the depositing of my payroll check, the paying of bills, etc. She guides our home as the Scripture says for the wife to do. I oversee all that she does, not to dictate to her, but just so that I can know what is going on and where we are financially. We agree on a decision and direction together before we come to a conclusion. We determined that it would be that way when we married twenty years ago. She has not taken employment for twenty years of our marriage.

We decided that because we wanted her to be home with our children while they were growing up. We thought it would be important for her to be there during those early years in the children's lives. We later found it is even more important that she be there at home during those adolescent years when they are coming of age. Our two children at home now are twenty-one and nineteen years of age. With the wisdom the Lord has given Theresa in handling our finances it allowed us to make it on just one salary in a time when it nearly demands two salaries in one household to make it. God gave to us men capable women who have skills in these areas. We must allow them to function in their gifts and abilities. This is another reason God used the term "help meet."

One of the reasons Black men do not like their wives to guide the house is because it has been embedded in their spirits not to do so. In most cases, as they were growing up, they heard their own fathers tell them, as well as other men, "Do not let your wife have any say in things. You are the man, so put your foot down and do not let no woman tell you what to do." I used to hear that you would be less than a man if a woman handled the money in your house. I used to believe that because that is what I used to hear before the Lord changed my life. What we have managed to do is to destroy a very important and powerful resource that has been given to us through marriage, the ability of the woman and her talents. Not all women are possessed with the ability to handle money well, but there are many other areas her skills are needed.

Another way that women guide their home is that they set the atmosphere in the home. I know that in my home if my wife is not happy, the whole house is unhappy. If she is not happy, the children are not happy; I am not happy, etc. On the other hand, if I am not happy, it seems to not bother anyone. The children get with their mother, and they are okay! And I'm the only one upset. Mothers, here is a very powerful truth that is the foundation of this book. You have the potential to guide your entire family into a life of success rather than failure. If you grasp the power you have and the influence you are, and couple that together with being in the position God wants you to be, it is endless what you can do with your husband and family.

"Give none occasion to the adversary to speak reproachfully." The Bible teaches in Proverbs 18:21 "that death and life is in the power of the tongue." What this means is that the words of our mouth have power to bring death or life to people or situations. If children hear only negative statements about themselves, then the drive to become something in life is assassinated by what is spoken. On the other hand, if positive things are spoken to children, then the drive to become something has been given the power of life. Eventually the child begins to believe in himself, and believes he or she is worth something in life.

I still remember a statement made about me to my mother by a friend of hers when I was just a boy that has never left my memory. Oftentimes it is played back in my mind, and it still has a profound effect on me physiologically. It was a very short and to the point statement, but it left a very positive impression in me about myself. This is what she said to my mother. Her name was Mrs. Gladys Bowser, and she used to fix my mothers hair. She said, "Carl Lee is going to be something one day." Carl Lee is what they called me in my neighborhood when I was very young.

She said that based upon what she thought of me. She did not even say it directly to me, and it has had a positive influence on me ever since. My mother repeated it to me, but she never knew what a profound effect it would have in my human spirit. The same thing can happen in a negative way if wrong words are spoken over children, or directly to them. Over the years oftentimes, when I would be down on myself to the point of having pity parties, I would be sustained by that statement from her about me. It revitalized me and helped me to recover.

Notice the apostle said give none occasion to the adversary; the adversary is the devil. His objective is to hurt, discredit, defame, destroy, and ruin young people before they find out their potential. The word reproachfully is used, and it means "a cause or occasion of blame, discredit, or disgrace." The continuing of that scripture reads in this manner, "Give none occasion to the adversary to speak reproachfully. For some are already turned aside after Satan."

This has been a problem throughout the history of Blacks in America, the act of speaking reproachfully. Most of us have done a great deal of speaking negative about one another. Satan takes advantage of our ill speaking, which is why the Word of God says "death and life is in the power of the tongue." By speaking the wrong thing, Satan takes what is said and uses it against individuals. Allow me to share with you what I believe the Lord brought to my memory as He caught me away in the Spirit. During those rough and bitter years of slavery, certain Black men were used as sex studs to produce strong healthy Black babies, to become strong healthy slaves. They would be chosen based on their health, strength, stature, and teeth. They would be paired with more than a few women to produce as many children as possible.

This type of activity would produce pride and competition among the male slaves. Another thing this action produced was a wrong message sent to young Black men as to what it meant to be a man. Because children learn by example, multitudes of young Black boys grew up thinking that in order to be considered a real man, they had to practice that type of sex. Still lurking in the minds of most young Black men, as well as some older men today, is the thought, *How many children you can make by different women determines whether you are a man.*

This helped caused the ill treatment of Black women everywhere then and now. So older women of that time who were abused by Black men, and some today still speak reproachfully of Black men. Sadly, much of the time the speaking is done in front of the young Black boys who will grow up to be men. Hearing all that negativity forms within him the mind-set that his father and other men were not worth very much. And that ultimately he will not be worth very much either.

That type of speaking "reproachfully" has aided in our present-day situations with our young Black men. Satan begins to work on the mental image of the young Black man because of what has already been said about him. He convinces the young man that he may as well go ahead and do whatever he wants to because he will never amount to anything anyway. And so many women have turned aside after Satan is speaking reproachfully in this way.

The devil goes on to to convince the Black man that the White man is his problem. The Black man does not understand that the word of reproach is what causes him to be defeated in all that he does. The devil will never tell that man he is not going anywhere because of what he believes. He reinforces the continual failure of Black men by convincing them to hate the White man. You will even hear Black men and women say that the White man is the devil. If the devil can convince us to continue to hate not only White men but anyone, we will never succeed in anything we attempt to accomplish.

The words that have been spoken reproachfully have helped to cause some Blacks to be where they are today. Never before in the history of America has there been more freedom for the Black man. Sadly today many are still enslaved in the spirit of their mind.

I want to reiterate: women have spoken reproachfully of Black men for a great number of years. Blacks have spoken reproachfully of one another for hundreds of years. The devil has merely taken our words and used them against us. This keeps the Black man distant and separated from one another with no respect and no trust.

Three

How Tradition and Religion
Have Affected Black America

From my earliest childhood memories of attending church and Vacation Bible school until I left the church I grew up attending at twenty-three years old, I do not remember a lesson taught or sermon preached on the family by the pastor or other ministers. There was only one time it happened in the church, that I was aware of and it was by a visiting preacher. I remember it so clearly for two reasons: number one was because the visiting preacher was a white man, which never happened before in the church, to my knowledge. The only time a white man spoke at the church was during election time, when white candidates came to speak to the congregation. They always had to leave right after they spoke a few favorable words and rush to another Black church.

The second reason was because I felt something I had never felt before. In retrospect, the preacher must have been saved and Spirit filled. I had never sensed what I sensed in that service that day. There is a term used among Black churches when the church service had a lot of excitement and enthusiasm. It's called "tore up." The people would say, "Boy, Reb. Tore it up today!" meaning he preached very well. Well, this white preacher "tore it up" that day. He preached on honoring women and mothers, and the family. When he finished preaching, he said, "Y'all need to honor your women and especially your mothers. Don't let the day end before you tell how much she means to you." Something came all over me, and later I learned that it was the Holy Spirit. Apparently it came over my brother also, because he experienced the same feeling.

My mother was not in service that day, so after service my oldest brother and I rushed home to tell our mother what had happened in church and what she meant to us. We were not used to hearing the Word of God proclaimed so boldly. We were used to hearing the old traditional whooping-style preaching. Consequently we were never taught how to live as a family, or how a father should love and honor his wife and children. Wives were never taught how to love and submit to their husbands, or how to raise children according to God's Word.

I recall as a child, while growing up, attending church services when a particular Sunday would be designated for the receiving of Communion. In the church I attended, Communion Sunday was the third Sunday of each month. On that Sunday more people attended services than any other Sunday of the month. It was due to how we were taught about receiving Communion. At the time I would hear adults make statements that they would not go out the Saturday night before third Sunday morning Communion Service. Of course "going out" meant a night of partying, drinking, carousing, and being promiscuous, etc.

Any other Saturday night would be acceptable to go out and participate in those kinds of activities. This type of activity was traditionally accepted in church, because many pastors have failed to instruct the congregation that this type of behavior was wrong for the Christian life-style. These people felt by not going out on the Saturday night before, that somehow helped them to be better prepared spiritually in order to take part in the service and receive Communion.

In the Bible, in chapter 15 of the book of Matthews, Jesus was in Jerusalem. The Scribes and Pharisees approached Him to ask a question of Him. Scribes were very knowledgeable concerning the Scriptures. They were writers and secretaries, men who copied the scriptures. Pharisees were a party among the Jews that laid great emphasis upon the observance of rites and ceremonies. They made a pretense of superior piety and separated themselves from the common people. They were believers in the immortality of the soul, the resurrection of the body, and the existence of angels and spirits.

They asked Jesus a question regarding His disciples breaking or not keeping a tradition in which they themselves were accustomed to keeping. They asked, "Why do your disciples transgress the tradition of the Elders? For they wash not their hands when they eat bread." The tradition they were referring to was something they obviously gave great adherence to. The word *tradition* means "the act of delivering over from one to another, anything handed down from the past, as from an ancestor or predecessor."

The tradition spoken of here was an act thought to have the ability to keep a person from being defiled by what they ate, and how they would eat. Jesus answered by saying, "Why do you transgress the commandment of God by your tradition?" Jesus went on to to say, "For God commanded, saying, Honour thy father and mother: and, He that curseth father or mother, let him die the death. But ye say, Whosoever shall say to his father or his mother, It is a gift, by whatsoever thou mightiest be profited by me; and honour not his father or his mother, he shall be free. Thus have ye made the commandment of God of none effect by your tradition."

There were two issues Jesus was dealing with regarding their traditional beliefs. When God's Word says to honor your father and mother, it means to not only give respect, but to also support them financially if need be. When it was said, "He that (curseth) father or mother, let him die the death." He was saying if one was to disrespect his parents, and refuse to support them if it is possible for them to do so, then they should be put to death according to God's commandment. Jesus went on to say, "But ye say" this is what your tradition demanded above what God said. "Whosoever shall say to his father or his mother, it is a gift, by whatsoever thou mightiest be profited by me."

What this statement means is that anything of mine that you might have been helped by has been given to God, (meaning given to them who was supposed to represent God) and he is not to honor his father or his mother. In other words, they do not have to do what

God's commandment says because your beliefs differ. Jesus in turn says, "You have made the commandment of God of none effect" by your beliefs in your traditions.

Jesus then went on to explain that the washing of the hands, which they put great emphasis on in the keeping of their traditional beliefs, was not important at all. In verse 11 He says, "Not that which goeth into the mouth defileth a man; but that which cometh out of the mouth defileth a man." In verse 18 Jesus states, "But those things which proceed out of the mouth come forth from the heart; and they defile the man." In Matthew 12:34, Jesus says, "For out of the abundance of the heart the mouth speaketh." What defiles a man is what is in his heart, because whatever issues are in his heart will be spoken out of his mouth, and that is what defiles men. Not simply the washing of the hands before eating. A good illustration of this is when someone is speaking and they mistakenly say something they did not intend to say. That person will generally say, "I did not intend to say that," and that may very well be true that they did not intend to say it. But it was in their heart, and it will eventually come out of their mouth.

Jesus said this regarding those who put their beliefs in their traditions above what God says. In verses 7-9, He says, "Ye hypocrites, well did Isaiah prophesy of you saying, This people draweth nigh unto me with their mouth, and honoureth me with their lips; but their heart is far from me. But in vain they do worship me, teaching for doctrines the commandments of men."

It is very possible to worship God in vain by adhering to traditional teachings about God and putting aside the very things God has said of himself. There have been traditional teachings about God handed down for many generations within the Black communities of America. Many of these teachings have been successful in keeping Black people from entering into a intimate biblical relationship with Almighty God. Ultimately it has kept them from reaching their full potential and purpose of God as a people.

Much of this was the case during the years when Blacks were enslaved; they could not read. The only knowledge the Black man received about God came from the traditional beliefs handed down to him by his forefathers. There were times when they were told things about God by those masters who actually cared for their slaves. Most of what they were taught was based upon traditional beliefs. But most of those things told to them by their master were true by the Word of God.

Jesus said, "Ye shall know the truth, and the truth shall make you free." I would like to add to this statement to what Jesus said, "The truth that you know shall make you free." If you do not know the truth, then the truth cannot make you free. There are so many churches where "The Truth" is not being taught; instead they are following traditional beliefs. If one adheres to religious and traditional beliefs over "the truth," then you will never experience the truth making you free as Jesus said.

There are different types of being set free we need to consider. Abraham Lincoln's Emancipation Proclamation is what began setting slaves free in 1862. Although it was not President Lincoln's primary goal to do, it piggybacked on him as he tried to preserve the Union army. That could not be done without the inclusion of the Emancipation Proclamation. The Black man became free as a part of that Proclamation. Even though he was made free by the Proclamation, he still had no civil freedoms. He could not eat where he wanted to; he could not live or work where he wanted; and the restrictions continued. Neither did he experience the kind of freedom that Jesus spoke of that the truth would ultimately bring.

In more recent times Blacks have been successful in obtaining civil freedom spearheaded by Dr. Martin Luther King Jr. The kinds of freedom that came with civil rights were being able to work, eat, live, and vote, along with many other freedoms. But not the kind of freedom Jesus spoke about. The winning of the battle over civil rights did bring much needed freedom, and indeed was a battle that had to be fought, and needed to be won.

But the Black man still did not experience the kind of freedom Jesus was speaking about. The type of freedom Jesus was talking about was spiritual freedom from the power and effects of sin in one's life. Spiritual freedom cannot be obtained by adhering to the traditional teachings and beliefs of one's predecessors. Ultimately, those teachings have made the Word of God, which can make him free spiritually, of none-effect.

Some of the religious traditions taught have been handed down for centuries. They were handed down as truth that would help make Blacks spiritually free. But, in all actuality, they have not made Blacks free, but instead have put the Black man into spiritual bondage. Let's take a look at some of these traditional teachings that have been handed down for quite some time now. I will only address those teachings as I myself have heard and experienced them in my growing up. One of perhaps the most fundamental teachings was how to become a Christian!

There is that old saying, "You need to join church, and do good." By this it was meant: when they say the doors of the church are open, go to the altar, shake the preacher's hand, and join the church by your Christian experience if you had any. Commit yourself to the church, and then commit yourself to work in the church. Then remain faithful to just go to church on Sundays, and you will be all right with God.

Of course after joining the church you were to sit on what was called "the Mourners Bench." This is not practiced anymore, but it was practiced for a long time. You would sit on a pew after joining the church and become a candidate for water baptism. You would stay there until you had a dream or some kind of spiritual experience. The young boys would wear a white handkerchief around their arm, and the young girls would wear a handkerchief around their forehead. This was to be an acknowledgment that they were candidates for salvation by water baptism. They would usually sit on the first row of pews in the church. You would have to sit there until God was supposed to speak to you in some way, by dream, or vision, or audibly. Then you would testify as to what you believe was revealed to you. Then you would go ahead and get water baptized, which according to the church was supposed to save your soul.

Then there is the teaching of "unconditional eternal security" taught in most churches. This teaching says that once an individual joined church, baptized, and became a member, they could never again be lost or fall into an unsaved position regardless of what they did. It was taught that once you went through the process of joining the church and being water baptized that you could never be lost or fall into an unsecured state again.

Do you remember perhaps the most familiar scripture in the entire Bible, John 3:16? "For God so loved the world, that he gave his only begotten Son, that whosoever believeth in him [should] not perish, but have everlasting life." The word *should* here is a verb, and it means that you "ought to" not perish, but the connotation here is that you could perish, but that you should not!

The prevailing thought was, after you get water baptized, then your life was supposed to change. Then you were to just be faithful to attend church. And when you would commit a sin God was to understand you were just a human being and you could not help but sin. Then He would forgive whenever we sinned. Now it is true that God will forgive whenever sin is committed if forgiveness is asked for after repentance. But the Lord does not want us to continue to sin, predicated on the fact that He will forgive. The difference is that the church thinks that you can continue to commit the same sin over and over, and God will forgive, based on the fact that you are just human and make mistakes.

Do you remember the woman caught in the act of adultery? Jesus did not condemn the woman, but He told her to go and sin no more. In the book of Matthew, chapter 1, verse 21, it says, "And she shall bring forth a son, and thou shalt call his name Jesus; for he shall save his people from their sins." Did you notice that it said "save his people from their sins": It did not say "in their sins." As long as the church believes that it can just live in sin because God will simply forgive, it will continue to be misled, blind leaders of the blind!

With this kind of traditional belief in mind, there is no real need for anyone to change his or her behavior. Therefore the church would accept a way of life that God himself opposes. Such as those who are living together without the benefit of marriage see no real need to change their situation. It used to be called "shacking up," and everyone knew it was wrong to do. But because it was traditionally believed that we were just human beings and could not help ourselves but to sin, it became acceptable to the church as a way of life. This has contributed to the birth of hundreds of thousands of children from illegitimate relationships. And when the couple got tired of each other, they just went their separate ways, leaving children without their biological parents and the security of the home they were born in.

In many of our traditional Black churches, it is still acceptable by the church to be sexually active before marriage. In addition to that, it is still permissible to live together without being legally married. I do understand that this is acceptable in society today, but it has never been acceptable as far as God and His Word are concerned. As a result of these permissible actions by the church, we continue to have children born from illegitimate relationships. The children themselves are not illegitimate, just the relationship that brought them into this world.

We continue to have very young girls having babies as a result of thinking it is okay to be sexually active while not being married. The church accepts it, and they see their parents and others participating, so in their thinking it is okay. We also continue to produce young Black men who think that you are not really a man unless you have as many babies and young women as possible. Then they think they have the right to brag about how much of a man they really are. I personally remember having it told to me time and time again by older men that you are not a man unless you are having as many young women as possible. And when it was not spoken directly to me, I would often overhear it in my presence.

Consequently, young men would go on the prowl looking for as many willing participants as possible. Young men and young women alike were taught that you had to have sex: We were taught that if you did not, you would literally eventually go crazy because of a natural desire for sex. Most of these beliefs came from right within the church.

Sin has a way of escalating. It will never stay stagnate. Because of this I believe we are experiencing some of the most dangerous times as Black Americans. We are losing our young men. We have an epidemic in our communities now with homosexuality, drugs, and AIDS. Never before have so many young Black men given into homosexual activity and life-style. Churches are accepting the homosexual life-style as an alternate and acceptable way to live. I can understand the world accepting homosexuality, but not the church. God does not accept it, and neither should the church. God and the homosexual life-style are diametrically opposed to one another. God does not hate those poor miss-guided souls who believe they were created to do what they are doing. He loves them and so should the church.

But to accept it as the way they should be is wrong! AIDS is at epidemic proportions in the Black community; because of this many Black men and women who participate in homosexuality are migrating toward drugs to help them deal with the pain of it all. There is nothing "gay" about the homosexual life-style. It is all about sex acts, which leave men and women feeling degraded and dirty. This causes them to feel the need for relief from all the psychological pain, so they turn to alcohol and drugs for relief.

I want to interject a thought here that helps explains perhaps why some young men and young women feel as though they are homosexual. I am in no way suggesting that I have a medical background or training in medical science. But it is written in medical books that the pituitary gland in a human being can malfunction and produce more estrogen in males and cause them to have feminine traits. And women can have more testosterone, which produces more male hormones and characteristics in their mannerism. This in itself does not cause individuals to become homosexuals or lesbians, but it may influence them to make the decision to choose to go that way in life. Let me see if I can better explain how this may occur. A little boy may have too much estrogen in his body due to a pituitary gland malfunction, which, by the way, can be corrected by a medical doctor. While he is growing up, other kids tease him because he is not as masculine as they may be. Or in some cases he may have been teased by girls for the same reasons. This alienates the child and he becomes lonesome and wounded emotionally. He begins to believe that something is wrong with him, and ultimately he accepts that he is homosexual only because someone suggests that he is.

As the child gets older he or she will find other children who may be experiencing some of the same things. Then they draw to one another for security and friendship. They do not fit in with other kids, so they begin to accept that they are different. But because they may not understand that it is a gland problem and there is help for it, they make the decision to follow after the homosexual life-style. There is a spiritual side to this life-style that no one likes to deal with, or they just shrug their shoulders and say it doesn't exist. I'm talking about demon spirits that convince people to do horrid things to themselves and others. They are a contributing factor to this alternate life-style and convince people that God created them the way that they are. The church must get involved and preach the truth so people can be delivered and set free.

Before I came to know the Lord, I was married at twenty-one, I remember during my first marriage we were having real problems, and I was the majority of the problems. I did not know what it meant to be a husband, so I went to talk to the pastor of a particular church. I told him of all the things we were going through in our marital relationship. The pastor suggested that I create a triangle in my relationship, by bringing a third party into our relationship, which in my case meant another woman. He said to me you have to do what you have to do in order to make it. I was not a Christian at that time, but even I knew that having an affair was not the answer to my problems. This was why I was having problems initially. But if the church teaches that this type of living is correct, is it any wonder why we're having the problems we're having in our lives?

Perhaps what I am about to share next is probably the most widespread of all teachings handed down, because the effects are still prevalent in the minds of most Blacks and evident in our communities today. It was said from the pulpits of most churches as well in conversations with friends and neighbors. In the minds of most Blacks prior to the integration of public schools was the pernicious thought that the White man was the devil. Of course the term did not suggest that he was the literal devil, but that he was just like the devil.

Some may find this hard to accept, but it is still going on today. "It is tough for me to write at this point, for I know how some Blacks may feel about what I am disclosing, but I must expound on this that perhaps some might get free of this self-imposed bondage." The Muslims or the Nation of Islam speaks publicly of what used to be said privately. So deep within the minds and spirits of most Blacks, and particularly elderly Blacks, is this false belief. The devil, through ignorance and hatred, causes Blacks to sink further into this self-imposed bondage.

On the lips of almost every Black person I ever heard while growing up was, "It was the White man that is keeping us down." The hatred in our hearts toward Whites, and the very thought that they were, are what is really keeping Blacks back. Allow me to explain why I say it is a self-imposed bondage. At the end of His model prayer, Jesus taught His disciples to pray. He gave them this instruction about the condition of their heart when they pray. In Matthew 6:14,15, it says, "For if you forgive men their trespasses, your heavenly father will also forgive you: But if you forgive not men their trespasses, neither will your Father forgive your trespasses."

What a profound truth! The devil himself knows that truth. So if we have been taught that the White man is the devil, how can Blacks ever get around to forgiving them for their trespasses? There has been much abuse of the Black man by White men. I do not think anyone can deny that this was actually the case with ill treatment. There is no need to go into detail. I believe everyone knows about our horrid past. But all that was done to Blacks was done because of ignorance and hatred by White men fueled by the devil. The devil wanted to destroy a powerful race of people before they could measure up to their full potential and purpose of God. How better to do this than to inflict pain, suffering, and even death, and then cause them to walk in unforgiveness.

The devil capitalized on both the White and the Black man's ignorance and hatred. The Black man, being the victim of such ill treatment, began to hate the White man. By so doing he himself went into bondage spiritually. This belief has been handed down through the Black community for as long as Blacks have been in slavery. And we have been in bondage to it ever since. Allow me to say it in no indecisive terms, "The White man is not the devil, nor is any other human being. The devil is a very real being, but he is a spirit being. While it is true he does use men against men, there is only one devil." And the White man and no other human being can hold the Black man or any man down who trusts in the God of Abraham, Isaac, and Jacob.

No man can keep anyone back regardless of his race, or for any other reason, if that person is in right relationship with God. Romans 8:31 says, "What shall we then say to these things? If God be for us, who can be against us?" This tells me that my success or failure does not depend on what color my skin is, or what my background may be, or who I know in the sense of rubbing shoulders with the right people. My success or my getting ahead is solely based on my relationship with Almighty God. I would like to apply a statement by Dr. Martin Luther King Jr., as it applies to Blacks who want to get ahead. He said, "The doctrine of Black supremacy is just as evil as the doctrine of White supremacy." So, should Blacks be elevated to a position of authority or the majority? They must remember that reverse racism is just as evil.

The history of the people of Israel in the Bible makes for a good illustration of the point I am trying to make. Some perhaps may remember it better by the movie Charlton Heston starred in as Moses in the *Ten Commandments*. Pharaoh, the most powerful man in the world, would have loved to have kept Israel, the people of God, in bondage as slaves, but when the Israelites obeyed God, Pharaoh could no longer hold them back as slaves. Because when God be for you who can be against you?

In recent times, Dr. Martin Luther King Jr. demonstrated this in America, during a time when it was very difficult to live as a Black man. His nonviolent approach could have only come from a heart of forgiving those who wronged him. No one can deny the effect he had on this country of America. When many other Blacks wanted to join his efforts and assist with violence, he rejected their help, because he knew that they would hinder God's help if he were to involve himself in anything that was contrary to the will of God.

It must have been a very lonely walk during those times for Dr. King, because few really understood what he was doing. But I thank God because he demonstrated what Romans 8:23 says, "If God be for you, who can be against you?" Some may sneer and suggest, "Well, he got assassinated!" Have we not yet realized that the cost to gain freedom has always come with a very high price, in many cases death? Dr. King lost his life for civil rights. Many Blacks in olden times lost their lives for the freedom to vote. President John F. Kennedy lost his life because of his views in regards to race relations. These are examples of freedom gained at the great price of death for civil freedom. But the ultimate freedom is spiritual freedom; it also came with a dear price as well. Jesus Christ, the Son of Almighty God, gave His life that we all might go free from the bondage and the effects of sin.

Four

How Ignorance and Hatred Keep Black America in Bondage

When will it end? Blacks as a people have been called Negro, Nigger, Colored, Black, People of Color, and now African Americans. Incidentally, please allow me just a few words to address how Blacks are now being addressed as African Americans. I am Black and have never considered myself to be an African American. I understand why we are called that, due to fact that our ancestors were being brought to America from Africa. I have never been to Africa and have no desire to live there.

I understand and accept that they are my ancestors, and I am proud of that fact. What I am expressing in no way suggests that I am ashamed of who I am because of where my ancestors came from, and what they went through. But the truth is, I am an American born in the United States of America and raised in this nation. I am just as proud to be an American as I am to be Black. There are some White people who now live in this country who may feel a little offended that only Blacks are called African Americans. Especially considering the fact that their homeland is Africa also, and they are not at all considered African Americans.

All of these titles, as far as I am concerned, are used incorrectly in trying to determine who I am and who all Blacks are. I am a Black American man whose ancestors came from Africa, whose roots, now that I have accepted Jesus Christ, go much farther than Africa. My roots now tie in with God Almighty through His Son Jesus Christ, and I am far more proud of that heritage than I am to be American or Black.

Webster's dictionary defines the word *ignorance* as "the lack of knowledge or learning." Referring once again to the time of slavery in America, Blacks were brought to this country from their native homeland of Africa. Because of ignorance it has been extremely difficult for Blacks to keep up on an intellectual scale with Whites for many, many years, I am speaking of earlier years in the eighteenth, nineteenth, and early twentieth century. If Affirmative Action needs validation, it should be based on this truth alone. Because of the Black man's beginnings in America, they were already several steps, if not miles, behind the White man as far as intellect is concerned.

After President Lincoln introduced the Emancipation Proclamation, he spoke before an audience of free Black leaders at the White House in mid-August 1862. Lincoln urged establishing a colony in Central America to which emancipated Blacks could emigrate. The President said that "even once they were free, Blacks would face a difficult time achieving equality in the United States: There is an unwillingness on the part of our people, harsh as it may be, for free colored people to remain among us." (A statement taking from the book *Lincoln and the Abolition of Slavery*, published by Lucent Books.)

History has already proven to us that starting out that far behind White people cannot be made up in a short period of time. So because the Black man now has access to higher education, he has gradually advanced through the years. He is able to compete on an intellectual scale, where as before he was not even in the game. But he has had to work extremely hard to overcome his much frustrated beginnings.

I would dare to say there are still many Blacks who feel hindered because of a lack of ability to fully exercise their minds. As opposed to children belonging to White parents who have always had the benefit of understanding the culture and the opportunity to acquire educational and intellectual skills. Let me see if I can simplify what I am saying! Because of the lack of intellectual preparation, in the past

Blacks found it very difficult to keep up on an intellectual scale. When parents at home began to prepare their children for school, they did not have a very good start intellectually, as opposed to White children who were prepared at a very early age to go into public education.

The Black child had been grossly undeveloped intellectually and not prepared for public education at all. So while the child belonging to a White family was being developed in his or her home, the Black child had to wait until they went to school to even begin to develop intellectually. This was largely due to the fact that Black parents were uneducated because of being denied the right to get an education for many years prior to their release from slavery. So even after being made free from slavery, they struggled on an intellectual scale. So when they were finally admitted to public schools, kids were coming from families who had no prior training or teachings at all.

If you can began to imagine trying to progress in a society that was not designed for you to participate in, you can understand why it has taken the Black man over two hundred years to begin to compete intellectually. We were never dumb, just ignorant. I am sure this is how the thought came about that White men were superior to Black men. I am so very proud to belong to a race of people that has that kind of fortitude and has come forth as we have by the help and grace of Almighty God, considering our most difficult and degrading beginning. It is a sight for sore eyes to behold if we can embrace our history where we have come from, and see where we are today. Now the potential we have is unlimited. Glory to God, it should make Black people want to shout!

Webster's dictionary defines the word *hate* as "to dislike intensely or passionately, to feel extreme aversion for, or extreme hostility toward." Found in the heart of many Black Americans is the definition of hate. While hatred is never accepted as right, it is certainly understandable how it can enter the heart of human beings of all races and nationalities, especially Blacks. To have experienced the kind of suffering and anguish Blacks have in America, it is understandable, but it is still wrong.

Hatred puts the individual who allows it to dwell in their heart to be in bondage to it. Then they become partakers of the person's actions against them and become like the person who perpetrated the act against them. That is why the Lord says to forgive them that have wronged you. In forgiving someone you choose not to hold the person or people to what they did. In the process you either keep yourself from going into the bondage of hate, or you release yourself from it because you were in bondage to it.

While Blacks were in their homeland of Africa, there was no knowledge of the God of Abraham, Isaac, and Jacob. This was the God that America was worshiping during the time of slavery. This was also the God of those who founded America were worshiping when searching for a country to freely express their worship, which was how America was discovered by the White man. I am not suggesting that the White man was the first to discover America, but they were looking for a place to express their worship freely to this God without opposition.

In Africa at the time of the capturing of slaves, there was the worship of other gods and demonic spirits. When men, women, and children began to be taken from Africa, obviously they did not want to come voluntarily. Not all were caught and taken. Some were even sold by those who were considered leaders in African countries. It would stand to reason why they would hate the White man, for all that was happening to them, and what would eventually happen to them when they would arrive in America.

As ugly and as gruesome as it was for Blacks during those years of slavery, I believe it was all a part of the divine plan of God. Let me say it this way. It was God's plan for the Black men, women, and children to be brought to this country. He allowed the Black man to come as he did. Many may be asking, how in the round world can this be? First of all, let me explain that Blacks would not have come to America freely of their own will. Secondarily, God wanted to bring Blacks here for a specific purpose, which I will attempt to explain.

There is a saying commonly used around most churches that "God works in mysterious ways." To be totally honest with you, this is not at all an accurate statement. The Bible says God does nothing without informing those whom he calls His friends. In the book of Amos 3:7, it says, "Surely the Lord God will do nothing, but he revealeth his secrets unto his servants the prophets." In the New Testament in the book of Ephesians 3:4-5 the apostle Paul writes this: "Whereby, when ye read, ye may understand my knowledge in the mystery of Christ which in other ages was not made known unto the sons of men, as it is now revealed unto his holy apostles and prophets by the Spirit."

So God does little without letting someone know what He is about to do. Remember before God would allow it to rain forty days and forty nights He told Noah? Remember He told Abraham that His people Israel would go into bondage for four hundred years? Isaiah prophesied that a virgin would give birth to a son who would be named Jesus; and many other events God informed men what He would do.

So if God intended for the Black man to be in America, it should be substantiated somewhere in the Word of God. I believe we can find just such confirmation of that fact in the book of Acts. Luke, who was a physician wrote, the Acts of the Apostles; who also was an apostle of the Lord Jesus Christ. God revealed the contents of the book of Acts to him. That God had made of one blood all nations of men, and determined where they would exist on the earth.

Let's read it the way Luke said it in the book of Acts, 17:24-27. "God that made the world and all things therein, seeing that he is Lord of heaven and earth, dwelleth not in temples made with hands; Neither is worshipped with men's hands, as though he needed any thing, seeing he giveth to all life, and breath, and all things; And hath made of one blood all nations of men for to dwell on all the face of the earth, and hath determined the times before appointed, and the bounds of their habitation; That they should seek the Lord, if haply they might feel after him, and find him, though he be not far from every one of us."

Please allow me to give the same scripture from the New International Version of the Bible. Acts 17:24-27: "The God who made the world and everything in it is the Lord of heaven and earth and does not live in temples built by hands. And he is not served by human hands, as if he needed anything, because he himself gives all men life and breath and everything else. From one man he made every nation of men, that they should inhabit the whole earth; and he determined the times set for them and the exact places where they should live. God did this so that men would seek him and perhaps reach out for him and find him, though he is not far from each one of us."

It clearly states that God determined the times set for them, and the places where they should live on the earth. He also revealed why He would do it in that way. So that men might have the opportunity to seek after Him. While the Black man was in Africa, he was not seeking after God, but God was seeking after him. There was no knowledge of the God of Abraham, Isaac, and Jacob in Africa. There were various types of worship, but not Christianity.

America as a nation at one time was majority Christian. The very foundations of this nation were built on the Word of God. The very purpose for which this nation was founded was to have a country where God could be worshiped without opposition, which is why the Pilgrims sought for a country in the first place.

This is one thing that always troubled me when I thought of the history of America: "How could a Christian nation allow slavery to coexist with its freedom?" Well, when I see it in this light it makes sense to me now. The White man thought he was acting on his own volition when he went to Africa and took, and in some cases purchased, what he thought would only be free slave labor. But lo and behold, Almighty God had other plans. God used the White man to bring the Black man to America for a different purpose. God's purpose was that the Black man would seek after God in a Christian nation and find Him, and Praise God we did!

There are some Black religious movements that proclaim that Jesus is the God of the White man only, and that Blacks should have their own God. I have come to the understanding that the God of Abraham, Isaac, and Jacob, the Almighty God is not a God just for one people, but for all people, for there is only one true God and Father of our Lord Jesus. So God allowed the White man to go to Africa to acquire a people who were worshiping anything but God.

The beauty of it all is God did it simply because He loves all men, and He wanted Blacks as well as others to come to know Him as their Creator and God. How else could a people having no rights or privileges rise from the pits of slavery to become a free people? It seems to me that history has repeated itself! Remember when the children of Israel were in slavery for four hundred years? No one but God could have delivered them out of slavery. And it was no one but God who caused the chain of events to take place that caused Blacks to be delivered from the bondage of slavery.

Let's consider a few of the events put into action just prior to the freeing of Blacks from slavery. The information of reference comes from the book *Lincoln and the Abolition of Slavery* published by Lucent Books, Inc. Perhaps the single most influential voice arguing for freedom from slavery was Frederick Douglass, a former slave who rose to become a role model for a nation. He was born on February 7, 1817, in Maryland as Frederick Augustus Washington Baily, the son of a slave. In 1838 he escaped to New Bedford, Massachusetts, and took the last name Douglass. In 1841, he spontaneously addressed an antislavery convention in Nantucket, Massachusetts, and his oratory was so powerful that he was hired as a speaker for the Massachusetts Anti-Slavery society.

Douglass spoke against the evils of slavery both in America and abroad, helping to convert thousands to the abolitionist cause. He campaigned for Abraham Lincoln during the election of 1860. Once the Civil War began, Douglass continually pressed Lincoln and the North to use Black troops in the struggle. Two of Douglass's sons were in the all-Black 54th Massachusetts Regiment.

After Abraham Lincoln was elected President, the trials and tribulations he endured as chief executive, both in his personal and public life, he derived little joy from reaching the highest office of the land. Hounded by office-seekers, haunted by staggering casualty lists, besieged by problems stemming from the war, reviled and ridiculed by his opponents, Lincoln frequently felt isolated and trapped in the White House. "I am the loneliest man in America," he said after news of yet another Union military defeat.

As Lincoln searched desperately for a general who could match the Confederacy's wily Robert E. Lee, the Union armies were frequently beaten, and beaten badly. These losses affected the president deeply. After learning of the terrible slaughter of Union troops at the Battle of Fredericksburg, the president wrung his hands and moaned, **"What has God put me in this place for?"** When a similar carnage of Northern soldiers occurred at the battle of Chancellorsville, the distraught Lincoln cried, **"My God! This is more than I can endure!"** He was so inconsolable over the loss of life that Secretary of War Edwin Stanton feared he might commit suicide.

Lincoln said sadly, "If hell is not any worse than this, it has no terror for me." On July 13, 1862, the border-state politicians rejected his latest plea to embrace compensated, gradual emancipation. Gradual emancipation would pay slave owners for their losses, and slaves would be given the choice of beginning life anew in another country. That policy, however, earned Lincoln the scorn of both anti- and pro-slavery groups. Lincoln told Secretary of State William Seward and Secretary of the Navy Gideon Welles that, after thinking about it for weeks, he had decided to issue an emancipation proclamation that would unilaterally end slavery. Lincoln summed up his reasoning in one concise sentence that yet spoke volumes: **"We must free the slaves or be ourselves subdued."** When the Lord wants something done, He will put men in situations so that His will may be accomplished. Proverbs 21:1 says, "The Kings (President) heart is in the hand of the Lord, as the rivers of water: he turneth it whithersoever he will."

Lincoln went on to to say, "My paramount objective in this struggle is to save the Union, and is not either to save or to destroy slavery. If I could save the Union without freeing any slave, I would do it, and if I could save it by freeing all the slaves I would do it; and if I could save it by freeing some and leaving others alone I would also do that. What I do about slavery, and the colored race, I do because I believe it helps to save the union."

Quoting from the Word of God in the book of Proverbs 19:21: "There are many devices in a man's heart; nevertheless the counsel of the Lord, that shall stand." The word *counsel* in Hebrew means "purpose"; so it is the purpose of the Lord that will come forth, even when men have other intentions. President Abraham Lincoln may have wanted to save the Union Army, but Almighty God had another objective in mind: to free Blacks from slavery!

The devil, who is the enemy of all men, has used slavery against the Black man to keep him controlled in the spirit of his mind, ever since he has been freed from slavery. Even though we have managed to gain civil rights, the devil still keeps Blacks constrained by causing them to "hate" White men who were used by God to get us over here in the first place. Many Black people are still bitter, angry, and unforgiving of the White man because of what God allowed him to do.

The White man did not understand the purpose for which he was bringing the Black man to this country. Again, quoting from the book of Proverbs 19:21, it says, "There are many devices in a man's heart; nevertheless the counsel of the Lord, that shall stand." The Black man could not understand the purpose for which he was taken from his homeland. But God's divine plan had been set in motion and was going to be fulfilled.

I heard a preacher use the phrase I am about to use that goes like this, "If you do not understand the purpose of a thing, abuse is inevitable." Simply put, if you not understand what something is intended for, eventually you will abuse it. The White man did not understand the purpose for which he was taking the Black man. He thought he was to be used for slave labor only. The White man did not understand that God was in it and had a purpose for every human being He created. So consequently the White man did what is inevitable if you do not understand the purpose for something. He abused the Black man.

Interestingly enough, the Black man himself did not understand his purpose for being here in America. So when he finally became a free man, and not knowing his own purpose, he began to abuse himself and others like him. And still today he continues to abuse himself and others like him wondering, WHY AM I HERE? Blacks are murdering each other in their own neighborhoods; they are selling dope to one another, sleeping with one another's wives, raping their own children, and children of others, abusing their wives and families. Blacks make up a greater part of the prison population in America. We just cannot seem to get it together! It's not because the White man is keeping us down; it is because we have not yet come to understand the purpose for which we are here.

I heard this same preacher say, "If you want to understand the purpose of a thing, you must go to the creator of the thing." In order for the Black man to ultimately understand his purpose, he will have to go to the One who created him. This is the very reason that God allowed Blacks to come to America, that we might seek after Him and find our purpose. Going back to Africa will not help us find our purpose; searching out our roots will only confuse us more. Finding our way home to God should be our ultimate determination and destination.

Five

What Is God's Purpose for the Black Man in America

Have you ever had the moment in your life when you asked yourself, "What am I doing here?" It is a question I believe every human being at some point asks in regards to why are they even alive, and why were they born! If you are Black, then it becomes a two-fold question. I believe everyone that is Black asks, "Why was I born, and why am I in America?" It is a discouraging question for the Black man, because of the way we came to America as a people. We came bound in chains on slave ships. Was there and is there an ultimate purpose for this?

Referring once again to the Bible in the book of Acts 17:24,27, I want to expound just a little further on this scripture. "**God that made the world and all things therein, seeing that he is the Lord of heaven and earth, dwelleth not in temples made with hands; Neither is worshipped with men's hands, as though he needed anything, seeing he giveth to all life, and breath, and all things. And made of one blood all the nations of men for to dwell on all the face of the earth, and hath determined the times before appointed, and the bounds of their habitation; That they should seek the Lord, if haply they might feel after him, and find him, though he be not far from every one of us.**"

"Dwelleth not in temples made with hands." In the Old Testament of the Bible, God dwelt in places built for Him by the hands of man. He instructed Moses to build a Tabernacle so He could dwell among His people Israel. In chapter 24 of the book of Exodus, Moses brought the people of Israel to mount Sinai. When they arrived God called Moses unto himself alone. During this visit God spoke to Moses to tell the people to bring offerings for the building of the Tabernacle. This is what the Lord told Moses in chapter 25:8:"And let them make me a sanctuary; that I may dwell among them."

Solomon was to build a temple for God, and it was a place where the presence of God dwells. But since then Jesus came and through His death made it possible for God to dwell in the heart of men now. The term *New Testament* means "the new covenant or agreement God established with man." The term *Old Testament* means "God's old covenant or agreement with man." Because Jesus made the new covenant possible, God no longer dwells in beautiful places of architectural design. His desire is to now dwell in the hearts of men. It reminds me of the worship song "Lord prepare me to be a sanctuary, pure and holy, tried and true; with thanksgiving, I'll be a living, sanctuary for you."

"Neither is worshipped with men's hands, as though he needed anything." God does not need anything from man. He wants man to worship Him; He does not need man to worship Him. God created man to worship Him. In the book of St. John 4:23-24, Jesus said this about worship: "But the hour cometh, and now is, when the true worshippers shall worship the Father in spirit and in truth: for the Father seeketh such to worship him. God is a Spirit: and they that worship him must worship him in spirit and in truth." This is why there is a desire for worship in the heart of every human being. Man's problem is that he wants to worship. He just does not know what to worship or how to worship.

Many people worship idols that are supposed to represent God. And those who fabricate these idols think that they are worshiping God by creating the idols. Many people worship buildings or sanctuaries that have been built for the worship of God. God cannot be worshiped by what man creates by his own hands. The Bible says

God is a Spirit, and they that worship God "must" worship Him in spirit and in truth. It is wonderful for man to worship God, but if man does not worship God, he will worship something else. And whatever man worships there is where his allegiance will be.

"Seeing he giveth to all life, and breath, and all things." Life comes from God; no other source can create life but God. God has given you life, and you are not a mistake. You were not accidentally created. The way you were conceived might have been unplanned, but make no mistake. You could not have life if it did not come from God. Many people use the term *illegitimate* children when a child is born out of wedlock. There are no "illegitimate" children only illegitimate relationships. So since you have life and you are not illegitimate, there is a purpose for which you were created. It makes no difference what your circumstances are, where you are in life, or what you do for a living, you have a purpose. God created you for a particular reason, and your life will never be complete until you discover what that reason is.

I say this because multitudes of people are hurting because of finding out how they were raised, or who their parents were, how they were conceived, or they may have even been adopted. And their whole life is hindered by the knowledge of what they may have found out. But we must go onto to seek out the purpose for which God gave us life. Then as we worship Him as we fulfill our purpose, then our lives take on the meaning and fulfillment God intended. In this we will discover what real peace and real joy really is. Ultimately, there will be no longer a need to hold to those things that happened years ago, or maybe even recently. You will finally be free of the burden and weight you have been carrying all these years.

"And made of one blood all nations of men, for to dwell on the face of the earth." Blood characterizes who our biological fathers are. I would like to use an analogy that you will need to use your imagination to understand. Suppose we set out to find out who our very first father was. It would begin something like this! You would start with a blood test, and from there you would match the blood of your father. Then you would match his blood with his father, then on to his grandfather and so on. If it were possible to continue to do this until you could trace back to the your very first father, guess who that would turn out to be? We would all discover that we all had the same first father; his name would be Adam. What a thought, "selah"; He made of one blood all nations of men. So all men were born of the same blood that flowed through Adam.

"And hath determined the times appointed, and the bounds of their habitation." God predestined and arranged the time that men should dwell on the earth, and He chose the specific location for them to be as a people. He chose when China, Russia, Germany, America, etc. would be inhabited. He also chose where in the world these and other continents would be located. God did all this. Make no mistake about the fact that God is responsible for where people are in the world today.

"That they should seek the Lord, if haply they might feel after him, and find him, though he be not far from everyone of us." It is the will of God that men seek after him. The term *if haply* is a Greek term that means "therefore accordingly, under these circumstances." The term *feel after him* is another Greek term that means "to grope," which means to search for as in a darken room searching for a light switch. "And find him, though he be not far from everyone of us."

God strategically puts people where He wants them so they as a people can seek after Him. In many cases He puts individuals where he wants them so that the individual would seek, or feel after God. Is there any other country that has all of the nationalities dwelling in it, as does America? There is a reason for this! That all men would seek after God in a nation whose very foundation began with adhering to the Judeo-Christian concepts found in the truth of the Word of God.

Such is the case with the Black man in America. God's ultimate purpose was for the Black man to seek after God. Notice in the last part of that verse it said that they "should seek the Lord." God will not make anyone seek after Him; although He could, He leaves it up to the individual whether or not he would. Only when an individual seeks and finds the Lord can his ultimate purpose be established. I use the term *ultimate purpose* because many people have a purpose, but it may not be the purpose for which God has planned for his life!

Referring back to statements made in the previous chapter, "If you do not know the purpose of a thing, abuse is inevitable." "If you wish to know the purpose of a thing, you must go to the manufacturer of the thing." If the Black man is to ever know his purpose for which he is in America and for which he has life, he will ultimately have to go to God, the One who created (manufactured) him.

Knowing that God is no respecter of persons according to Scripture, the purpose for which the Black man is in America is no different from the purpose of the White man, or any man in America. God wants every man to seek Him and find Him. As long as the Black man is unaware of the purpose for which God has Him here, he will always be in question about himself, where he is, and will never be able to fulfill his ultimate destiny.

When a man seeks after and finds God, he is to love the Lord with all his heart, soul, and mind, and to love his neighbor as himself. He is to raise his children in the fear of the Lord, and to instill the principles of God in his children. He is to do this so God's will can be established in the earth. Children in the Black communities of America have seen what traditional religion has done to many adults. Traditional religion tends to make hypocrites out of people. Jesus describes a religious person as one who serves God in vain by saying all the right things, but his heart is really far away from doing the things he says. This has caused children to be disenchanted with the so-called religious experience. So, in turn, they do not want anything to do with what they believe to be God as they grow up.

They have witnessed the joining of church by their parents, they have witnessed the water baptisms, and they have heard them say all the right things. But they continue to hear about racial prejudice, and the White man being the devil, and being held down by the White man. If he lies, his children will hear it. If they gossip, the children will hear it. If they hate, the children will know it. What happens to the God of the family? When the Black man seeks and finds God, and loves Him with all his heart, and walk in the ways of God, his children will come to know that God and follow in his footsteps. Children learn by example, not by what they have been told. Jeremiah 29:12-13 says,

"Then shall ye call upon me, and ye shall go and pray unto me, and I will hearken unto you. And ye shall seek me, and find me, **when ye shall search for me with all your heart.** When this occurs, the purpose for which the Black man is in America will resonate with him. Then his purpose can be realized, and his destiny can be aligned with God's ultimate purpose. Then the Black man comes to the reality of his purpose, and new life is born.

Six

Where Are Black Men Today in America?

I f the question were only dealing with the status, geographical, or the economical state of the Black man, the answer would be somewhat positive. But this book is not dealing with just the status, geographical, or economical state; it deals with the spiritual mental and psychological state of the Black man in America as well. Therefore, the answer to this question must be addressed in a meticulous manner. In order to be conclusive, it is incumbent that negatives be addressed as well as positives.

Quite a few years ago I remember being invited to speak to an all men's group that consisted of a predominately Black, if not an all Black, male group. As I sought the Lord as to what subject I should address, I believe He put this subject title in my spirit: "Men Lost in the Fallacy of Manhood." Webster's dictionary defines the word *fallacy* as "a deceptive, misleading, or false notion." For over two centuries Black men have lived under several fallacies of what it means to be a man.

Black men have always believed that it was right for them to be the head or leader in their homes and families. In fact, this teaching is correct that men should be the head of their homes. It can be founded in the Word of God. But this truth has been taken so out of context and made a fallacy. The way God intended for men to lead their families is altogether different from the fallacy that has been taught and taken out of context. It has been taught that the man of the house in a Black family was to be physically dominant over his wife and children.

This is the way that the average Black man still thinks today. It is deeply rooted in their minds, having been put there through erroneous teachings and even learned through observance. It even still lingers to some degree in the mind of the man who has given his life to the Lord. And for a Black man to be less than dominant, he was thought to be less than a man by his peers. It's an unspoken conviction, but it is there in the hearts and minds of most Black men.

So they set out to prove that they are men, armed with this fallacy. And in the process they have destroyed their homes with this fallacy and have destroyed many women and children, thereby destroying themselves. It was never God's intent that this happen. However, it is God's intent that men assume the role of the spiritual head of their homes. As priests were in the Old Testament of the Bible over the people of Israel, that is how God wants men to be priests or head of their homes. The priest of Israel was to represent God to the people, and to represent the people to God. So God intends for the man to spiritually represent his family to God, and to represent God to his family.

This does not imply that women and children cannot go to God for themselves as individuals. But for the man to walk as the head of his home, it is incumbent that he leads the family spiritually. His headship should be in a spiritual capacity. He should pray with and for his family. It took me years as the spiritual head of my home to come to this place of praying with my wife and children rather than being quick to instruct and direct.

Allow me to share with you some of my personal experiences. I have the tendency to tell Theresa how to correct or get out of a situation that she may be dealing with rather than listen and pray with her about it. She often tells me that I frustrate her more by offering advice rather than listening and making it a matter of prayer. Sometimes Theresa just wants me to hear what she is trying to say. The mentality I tend to exert is to solve the problem quickly. This mentality has been instrumental in leading into many arguments rather than me being a blessing to her.

There have been times when she would express fear about certain things. My thinking would be to tell her what the Word of God says about fear and how to handle it. This was no doubt a right way to handle the situation, but sometimes that is not what she is looking for. She knows what the Bible says about fear and how to handle it. She just wants me to hear her concerns. I have the tendency to do the same thing with my children, especially my son. He will begin sharing something with me and here comes the all-knowing wisdom of the head of the family. Before he finishes, many times I am already giving him answers to his dilemma. I guess I do that because I am the man and I am trying to be the head. I have come to realize that to be a good head or leader, one must be a good listener, be empathetic, and ask questions to show interest and concern. Boy, I wish I had the wisdom to do this when I am faced with it, as it sounds to me as I write!

When problems present challenges to the family, the head should assume the role of the leader and lead the family into the presence of God through prayer to get directions and answers as to how to find their way. In most of our homes and churches across America, women find themselves being the leaders in the home and church. They are taking on responsibilities that man should be doing as leaders in their homes and churches. Thank God for women who do step up to take the lead, because most men are absent when it comes to leading their family spiritually.

God intended for the man to serve his wife and children. By doing so he will represent God to his family. Many children and adults during their childhood had their representative as head of the family misrepresent his position as head, thereby causing the family (especially the children) to find it difficult to trust God. In the eyes of children, the father in the home is just like God to them when they are very young.

When children are very young, they believe in their fathers. They believe that he knows everything and cannot do anything wrong. When the father leads in such a way that the children cannot trust him, they find it very difficult to establish trust in the Lord to lead them as they grow older, especially little girls because of the closeness of the relationship. You see, the man in the family represents God whether he understands it or not. Therefore not knowing what God intended, the fallacy of manhood has ensnared literally millions of Black men for years.

Another fallacy that tends to ensnare Black men is "having sex and making babies makes you a man." I have heard and witnessed men and young men brag concerning the number of women who were impregnated at the same time by them. They would square their shoulders back and have a proud look on their face, as though they have done some great thing. Having sex and making babies does not and has never made anyone a man. I am sure you have heard that when a young person plans to have sex for the very first time, it is considered becoming a man or a woman. The fact that someone can engage in sexual intercourse and impregnate someone or become impregnated by someone only says that you are able to procreate. It does not make one a man or woman!

Because of this fallacy alone millions of children are born from illegitimate relationships, and millions of single mothers are left to struggle to raise children without the help of the fathers, financial assistance, or his presence. Then the young man, who believes he is a man because of what he has done, begins to dodge the responsibility of what it really means to be a father and a man. He does not support the child financially, and even in some cases he disowns the child so he cannot be made to support the child. God never intended for this to happen.

Alcohol and drug usage are other fallacies that have managed to cripple Black men. The general thought is "the more you can do, the more man you are." Young men are teased because they can only drink a couple of beers before they began to feel the effects. So the young man goes about trying to earn the reputation of being a man. "A man should be able to handle his drink" some would say! The very act of drinking has begun the downfall of many Black men today, and some have gone on to alcoholism.

Drugs are becoming more and more an epidemic in Black communities across America. The challenge to become a man, or to prove you are a man lies with whether you can handle your drugs or not, as some would say. Today, crack cocaine is destroying more homes and lives than alcohol in just a short period of time. But just as one would be pressured to drink to prove his manhood, likewise the testing with the drugs is the same if not a greater challenge.

Fighting and killing are still more fallacies. If you choose not to fight and walk away from a fight, then you would be considered less than a man. Many a young man set out to establish his reputation as entering manhood by fighting. In the process, he winds up taking someone's life or losing his life just to have it said he is a man, or spending a good portion in prison or some detention center, which in itself is another fallacy. I can remember while in high school when some young men would get locked up for one reason or another in a detention home. When he would be released, he would wear the experience as though it was a badge, and proof he was a man.

I am talking about fallacies that have held Black men bound to this way of thinking for years. This mind-set will ultimately keep him from ever accomplishing the purpose for which he was created. But God is about to change all this, hallelujah!! God is moving in the heart of Black men like never before. The Black man will come to God! He will respond to this fresh move of the Holy Spirit. He will embrace the truths of God's Word and become a threat to all that he helped to establish as fallacies of what a man is. He will walk away from all the fallacies that the devil is ultimately responsible for trying to hold him down that have been erected in his life.

As a result of the fallacies believed by Blacks, it has helped to cause increased numbers of Black males in our prison systems. The death toll on our streets of young Black males is higher than any percentage of any race or females. We must awaken to recognize what the devil has managed to do to Blacks. Through ignorance and deception the devil does not want us to know what our purpose really is, so Blacks can come to full potential as desired by God.

As stated earlier in this book, the devil has successfully caused the Black man to view the White man as his problem. Therefore, his plan to keep the Black man down has been protected so far. When are we going to arise out of sleep and overcome the devil? I caution you, this cannot be done until we surrender ourselves to God. As long as our lives are not given over to the Lord, the devil has a right to do almost whatever he wants to do, and we cannot stop him.

There is another fallacy that has far greater consequences than any that I have mentioned thus far. A fallacy that is more dangerous than the epidemic of drugs and the incurable disease called AIDS. This one fallacy alone is why many of our men and women cannot escape all the other fallacies mentioned earlier. It does more damage in the natural sense than AIDS and has an eternal punishment that comes along with it. AIDS, as dreadful as it is, has no cure for it at the time of this writing. The fallacy I am referring to now is far more dangerous than AIDS, but even though it has eternal consequences, thank God there is a cure for it. This fallacy I'm talking about is called "traditional religion."

Traditional religion has never brought anyone to a saving knowledge of Jesus Christ. Traditional religion has never freed anyone from the bondage of sin. It has never healed a crippled body, or raised anyone from a sick bed. It stops men from having a genuine experience with God. It has never gotten anyone into heaven, and it never will. And if it is relied upon to save one from hell, they will be hopelessly doomed to this place of torment. Traditional religion has done more to keep people separated and segregated than anything else. Also it has caused more people to go to hell than drugs, violence, bar rooms, crime, or anything we can imagine.

It is a common saying that "the most segregated hour in America is on a Sunday morning." Traditional religion has never freed anyone from being bound by anything. Quoting Jesus again He said, "You shall know the truth and the truth shall make you free." The Black man will never really be free until he comes to the knowledge of the truth, which is in Jesus Christ and not religion. When an individual is really set free from sin, he will be free from all things that have held him captive.

The Black man has been enslaved by his beliefs in traditional religion, as well as millions around the world, regardless of race or origin. Remember the word *fallacy* means "a deceptive, misleading, or false belief." There can be no greater fallacy than one that will cause a human being created in the image of God to be eternally separated from God at the time his life ceases to exist in this world. God did not bring the Black man to America to seek religion. He brought him here to seek after God. Some perhaps may ask the question, what is the difference?

Here are pretty good examples of traditional religions! Jehovah's Witnesses in their beliefs worship Jehovah, but they do not believe in heaven or hell, which Jesus himself spoke of often. The Catholics worship Mary and the Saints. They believe there is a place called purgatory. Purgatory does not exist. It is not mentioned anywhere in the bible. The Muslims believe that Ala is God. Buddhism believes that Buddha is God. The Baptist believes in unconditioned eternal security, once saved always saved. Pentecostals believe if you're not baptised in Jesus name you're going to hell. And there are many more religious beliefs. Which of these is the right religion? All of these cannot be right! I will tell you this: all of these beliefs are traditional religion in its truest form.

Jesus said, "I am the way, the truth, and the life, no man cometh unto the father but by me." There is but one way to get to God and to heaven, and that is through Jesus Christ. As long as Black people believe the fallacy of traditional religion, we will protest and teach our children the same tactics, which were handed down about hatred and retaliation.

So the question, "Where are our Black men today?" reverberates through the annals of our past and even comes to us today. A goodly number are still lost in the fallacy of manhood. As long as the Black clergy continues to teach that sex before marriage is acceptable, and living together without the benefit of marriage is okay. As long as they teach that drinking is socially acceptable. As long as they accept that homosexuality is a legitimate acceptable alternate life-style. As long as they teach church membership will ensure your passage to heaven.

As long as it comes from the pulpits that the White man is the devil. As long as Blacks do not understand their purpose for why God brought us here, all the fallacies that have been handed down to us will continue to engulf us and, consequently, the youth of Black communities. But God is beginning to shake us up and bring us to the knowledge of the truth. Then we will finally be able to say, free at last, free at last, thank God Almighty, we are free at last, according to the old Negro spiritual.

Seven

The Strength of Black America: Women, Why?

Can you imagine the strength of any people being squarely placed on the shoulders of a woman? What is it about a Black woman that God has called her the strength of her people. Can this strength be tapped into? What will she be able to do in America for her people? Will she accept the role and the responsibility? Can she overcome the years of abuse and neglect? The answer to these questions and even more possibilities are a resounding "yes she can" and "yes she will." The Lord is about to do an awesome work in the hearts and minds of Black women who will allow Him the freedom to do with her as He will.

In the Bible, in the book of Deuteronomy, the six chapter, just before Israel was to enter the Promised Land, God gave Israel specific instructions as to how to live and what to do as they were embarking upon beginning a new life free from the bonds of slavery. God gave them commandments, statues, and judgments to keep and to obey. Remember while in slavery they were given everything they had and told by the Egyptians everything they were to do. They did not know any more than what was given to them and demanded of them by those who enslaved them.

God gave them principles by which to live by, and included in those principles were training for the children. This is what God said to them in Deuteronomy 6:6-7: "And these words, which I command thee this day, shall be in thine heart: And thou shalt teach them diligently unto thy children, and shalt talk of them when thou sittest in thine house, and when thou walkest by the way, and when thou liest down, and when thou risest up." The godly principles referred to were intended to raise children to be strong in character and morality, and have a reverence for God and to know how to live as family and to serve the Lord with all their heart. These principles were to be adapted by the parents as a way of life, not just to be taught verbally, but to be demonstrated by example. Because children do not learn by what they are told by parents, they learn by observation of their parents' actions.

It is obvious there has been a breakdown of the teachings of God's principles in the day and time we live in America. This is one of the reasons women are considered The Strength of Black America. Women have the potential to reinstate the principles of God in the lives of their children. In almost every case, it is the woman who trains, equips, and prepares her children for life. The average woman spends the majority of her life with her children. Men tend to be more the disciplinarian and do not spend as much time with the children as do the women. So mothers have a real opportunity to implement things in the lives of her children that will last a lifetime; and in the case of training children in the things of God, it will last an eternity.

I have watched this in our home as Theresa has spent time with Lester and Miriam training them about the things of life and the things of God. While I was pastor of a church in New Iberia, Louisiana, our son lost all interest in school and was actually failing. We believe he would have dropped out of school if Theresa and I had not intervened. This was the year we decided to home school both our children. Theresa was very nervous about taking on this kind of responsibility, but we prayed together and she trusted the Lord to help her.

She began each day with prayer and, during the day, used discipline if necessary. I saw her rise to the occasion and accept the challenge of home schooling her children. She home schooled our son,

Lester, for four years. Throughout his high school career he went from failing to almost dropping out to honor roll. He graduated third in the class of 2,000 as an honor graduate. After graduating he enrolled in college as a freshmen in the fall semester of 2001. We did a full graduation ceremony for him: cap, gown, ring, and diploma, and friends and family were invited.

The principal of his home school program came to speak at his graduation. The theme for his graduation was "Is there not a cause?" Taking from the Bible when David took on Goliath the giant, he asked, "Is there not a cause?" After Lester received his diploma and made a speech thanking God for his mother's teachings and discipline and his father supporting her, I awarded Theresa with a framed certificate of excellence for a job well done. Our daughter, Miriam, will be graduating with the class of 2002. The Brown's Family Home School will be hosting another exciting graduation.

America's foundation and beginnings were established on the Word of God. Its principles have been handed down from generation to generation. Carved in stones in the monuments that are located in our nation's capitol is the Word of God. I remember walking through the monuments while on a visit to Washington, D.C., and I was awestruck that God's Word was engraved in the monuments' stone. Even on our currency is found the profound statement for America "In God We Trust."

Just recently in our country there was an issue about not saying "one nation under God" in the Pledge of Allegiance to the Flag. We cannot erect the Nativity scene on any government property. We do not even use the Bible in most courtrooms anymore. It is ironic that our schools were started with the Bible as its foundation book, and now you cannot even discuss the Lord in our schools. America is moving away from God. We want to enjoy the benefits of His grace, mercy, peace, and prosperity, but we do not want to acknowledge Him as God. We are more concerned for protecting the rights and privileges of our foreign population than to uphold the Lord as the God of America. What is going on? Are there any government officials willing to stand out and protest what's happening to the moral fiber of our once thriving nation?

Prayer used to start the day in our schools, and our government officials would open their sessions with prayer and ask for guidance.

In society today, this is no longer the case in our public schools, public buildings, governmental buildings, etc. And as a result we have left the principles God intended to build good morals, integrity, strong character, strong marriages, and strong family values. This has all been done to try to protect the sanctity of the Supreme Court's ruling separating Church and State. America in her efforts to protect this missguided law has managed to violate a greater law, a moral law, separating God and state. I do not believe our founding fathers who created the Constitution of the Untied States of America intended that the separation of Church and State would ultimately eliminate God from the state.

I would like to introduce some information I discovered regarding the wall separating between church and state in regards to the Constitution. I discovered this information in a book published by The National Center for Constitutional Studies. Its title is *The Making of America—The Substance and Meaning of the Constitution*, authored by W. Cleon Skousen.

On page 681, under the heading The "Wall" Between Church and the Federal State: "While Thomas Jefferson served in the Virginia legislature, he introduced a bill to have a day of fasting and prayer; but when he became President, Jefferson said there was no authority in the federal government to proclaim religious holidays. In a letter to the Danbury Baptist Association dated January 1, 1802 he explained his position and said the Constitution had created 'a wall of separation between Church and State.'"

In recent years the Supreme Court has used this metaphor as an excuse for meddling in the religious issues arising within the various states. It has not only presumed to take jurisdiction in these disputes, but it has actually forced the states to take the same hands-off position toward religious matters, even though this restriction originally applied to the federal government. This obvious distortion of the original intent of Jefferson (when he used the metaphor of a "wall" separating church and state) becomes entirely apparent when the statement and actions of Jefferson are examined in their historical context.

It will be recalled that Thomas Jefferson and James Madison were anxious that the states intervene in religious matters until there was equality among all religions and that all churches or religions assigned preferential treatment should be disestablished from such preferment. They further joined with the other founders in expressing an anxiety that all religions be encouraged in order to promote the moral fiber and religious tone of the people. This, of course, would be impossible if there were an impenetrable "wall" between church and state on the state level. Jefferson's "wall" was obviously intended only for the federal government, and the Supreme Court application of this metaphor to the states has come under severe critism.

Continuing to draw information from this extraordinary book *The Making of America*, I want to look at "Principle 215 from the First Amendment." Congress shall make no law respecting an establishment of religion, or prohibiting the free exercise thereof on page 676.

In 1787, the very year the Constitution was written by the Convention and approved by Congress, that same body of Congress passed the famous Northwest Territory. They also enunciated the basic rights of Citizens in language similar to that which was later incorporated in the Bill of Rights. And they emphasized the essential need to teach religion and morality in the schools. Here is the way they said it, Article 3; Religion, morality and knowledge, being necessary to good government and the happiness of mankind, schools and the means of education shall forever be encouraged.

We also notice that "religion and morality" were not required by the founders as merely an intellectual exercise, but they positively declared their conviction that these were essential ingredients needed for "good government and the happiness of mankind."

It was never the intent of our Founding Fathers who created the Constitution of the United States of America that there would ever be a "wall" separating church and state. The founders intended that there be separation from Congress and the federal government's involvement on a state level that involves the church, but they encouraged all religions to have their intended effect on society. No one described the effect that religion had on America better than the French Judge and Political Writer Alexis de Tocqueville.

Once again quoting from *The Making of America* under the heading, Alexis de Tocqueville discovers the importance of religion in America on page 678. When Alexis de Tocqueville visited the United

States in 1831, he became so impressed with what he saw that he went home to Europe and wrote "Democracy in America," one of the most definitive studies on the American culture and constitutional systems that had been published up to that time.

In America, he noted, the clergy remain politically separated from the government but nevertheless provide a moral stability among the people, which permits the government to prosper. In other words, there is a separation of church and state but not a separation of religion (God) and state.

In one of de Tocqueville's most frequently quoted passages, he wrote: "I sought for the greatness and genius of America in her commodious harbors and her ample rivers, and it was not there; in her fertile fields and boundless prairies, and it was not there; in her rich mines and her vast commerce, and it was not there. Not until I went to the churches of America and heard her pulpits aflame with righteousness did I understand the secret of her genius and power. America is great because she is good and if America ever ceases to be good, America will cease to be great." It is no secret that America is in real trouble because we are losing our greatness! Could it be possible that de Tocqueville's words are prophetic?

Whenever there is a lack of knowledge of God or an outright rejection of God in America or any country, it usually spells trouble. During the history of the advancement of Blacks, God's principles were never really instituted in the homes and lives of Blacks. There were some few homes that understood, but for the most part Blacks were ignorant of the principles and the word of God. Some may find it difficult to agree with this statement, but I believe that history and the present prove this statement to be accurate and true. Our roots and heritage were established in traditional religious beliefs and not in the truth of God's Word. This certainly does not mean that Black people did not love the Lord, nor did they not want to or try to live for Him. But without education they could not read with comprehension to understand God's principles in His Word, the Bible. Even though the Bible is not understood when read, as most books are, you at least need to know how to read to understand it.

As I make these statements, I do believe there were some Blacks who had been taught how to read by some White people that loved them, even though it was against the law. But there was not nearly enough to affect much of the Black population. This is in no way a plot or intent to discredit such a strong and prideful people, but to make factual statements that prove to be true and right. The reason why most Whites did not want Blacks to be educated was the fear that a revolution would begin if Blacks were to become sophisticated. Therefore, it was unlawful to teach Blacks how to read or write or give them educational material, including the Bible.

Generation after generation would come and go, and our forefathers were handing down traditional religious beliefs. As I referred to in an earlier chapter, in the book of Matthew, chapter 15, Jesus told the Scribes and Pharisees that their traditions made the Word of God of none effect in their lives. In the same sense, traditional religious beliefs that continue to linger to this day still make the Word of God of none effect. When the Bible says "make the word of God of none-effect," it means that if God says something will happen according to His Word; if we do something different to try to get the same results, it will not happen.

Please allow me to give the most critical of all examples as it relates to believing traditional teachings versus the truth of what God himself has said. I believe those of us who believe that there is a heaven and hell also believe there is nothing more important in human existence than which one a human being will eventually go to when they cease to exist in this life. In Matthew 14:6, Jesus says, "I am the way, the truth, and the life: no man cometh unto the Father, but by me." Of course, we all know that the father is God who is in heaven. Except an individual come to Jesus Christ for salvation, he cannot go to heaven when his life is ended on earth. If one tries to get to heaven by other means than what the Word of God says is the way to get to the Father, it will have no effect on that individual's life, and they will die and go to hell.

For two centuries traditional religious teachings have been handed down to Black women. about how to be a wife and mother. Some of the teachings have been detrimental to the well-being of the home and family. It is time that Black people learn to put away traditional teachings and find out how to apply the truth of God's Word to our lives. The Word of God tells how older women should teach the younger women.

In the book of Titus 2:3,5, it says, "The aged women likewise, that they be in behavior as becometh holiness, not false accusers, not given to much wine, teachers of good things; that they may teach the young women to be sober, to love their husbands, to love their children. To be discreet, chaste, keepers at home, good, obedient to their own husbands, that the word of God be not blasphemed." There is such power that women have to influence the lives of their husbands and children.

Black women must learn from God's Word how to apply this power and truth to their lives and use the power of influence in a positive manner. For many years children were taught things about God and about the church, because of what was traditionally believed, the information has not always been correct. Therefore because of tainted information being given, the results have produced more negatives than positives in the lives of Blacks.

In the book of Proverbs, chapter 22:6, it says, "Train up a child in the way that he should go, when he is old he will not depart from it." In other words, if we train our children according to God's Word, they will continue in that way. This does not imply that the child will always do the right thing as they are growing up, or even want to live for the Lord during adolescence. But He gives us an assuredness that if we train them properly, they will return to their foundation that was put in them. The story of the prodigal son demonstrates this for us. As the prodigal went out to experience life as he thought it should be for himself, he found himself in a downward spiral. As he painstakingly took account of where he was, he began to come back to the foundation put in him by his father.

Just imagine if we allow our children to grow up without teaching them biblical principles as foundations. They will not have that foundation to fall back on when they get in trouble in life, especially in the times we now live. You can be assured that in today's time, young people have much more of an opportunity to be carried away than young people in a previous time. And they will come to a point in their lives when they will face these temptations.

There are many and varied devices to try to ensnare young people today. When they pursue those devices and get ensnared, eventually they will want to get out, but if they do not have a strong biblical foundation of truth, they may very well find themselves in a no-win situation. This is when parents lose their children absolutely. The child may feel hopeless and some cases contemplate suicide, because of feeling overwhelmed by circumstances.

Because of their traditional religious beliefs, parents in Black communities thought they were raising their children in the way they should go. They took their children to church at very early ages. They would have them baptized and join the church as children. When they grew older, the children would get bored with just attending church and leave the church and never return. Parents would then wonder why their children would stop attending church. When the children would fall into that downward spiral, they would not know how to get out, and they would cease to attend church. They knew that it would take more than just attending church to help them. Then they would not have the foundation needed within them to fall back on.

Without proper understanding, parents tried to get their children involved in a traditional religious movement and the traditional teachings of the church. Remember what Jesus said in Matthew: your traditions have made the Word of God of none effect. Therefore, instead of the children getting a foundation of truth that will ultimately keep them as they get older, they were getting a foundation based on traditional religious beliefs that cancels any truth that Jesus taught. This rendered the Word of God "that the children would not depart" ineffectual in the lives of those who were taught traditional religious foundations.

Because of this, many young Black men has failed as the head of his home and family because of a lack of knowledge of God. He was never really taught the Word of God about what God expected of him as a Christian man, a husband, or a father. In the process he has abused his family and, particularly, his wife, and in many cases he has abused his role in the training of his children. This ultimately caused the Black woman not to want to be submissive to her husband, which being submissive is in accordance to the Word and the will of God. But because of the abuse, she felt she had no other choice, so instead of training her children in the nurture and admonition of the Lord, she has trained them according to the traditional religious teachings that oppose the Word of God.

The Black woman in obedience to God's Word is in a position of power to shape and mold her children, as well as her husband. What she does in this position as a woman determines whether the influence she has will be positive or negative in the lives of her husband and children. The positive can only happen when the principles of God are instituted.

God is calling on Black women to save the young Black males from becoming victims of the fallacy of manhood. God has called on women before to save male children from being put in danger. In the book of Exodus, chapter 1 a new Pharaoh took over in Egypt and did not know Joseph and the people of Israel. Israel had been allowed to dwell in Egypt by the previous Pharaoh. But when the new Pharaoh began to reign, he feared that Israel would outnumber the Egyptians and cause a revolution, so he made them slaves. And in order to control the number of Israelites being born, he issued an order that every male child that would be born was to be put to death.

This is what the Scripture says in Exodus 1:15,17: "And the King of Egypt spake to the Hebrew midwives, of which the name of the one was Shiphrah, and the name of the other Puah: And he said, When you do the office of a midwife to the Hebrew women, and see them upon the stools; if it be a son, then ye shall kill him: but if it be a daughter, then she shall live. But the midwives feared God, and did not as the king of Egypt commanded them, but saved the men children alive."

Thank God those midwives loved God more than anything else, or God's plan would not have worked. Incidentally, one of the young baby boys saved from death was Moses, who went on to deliver Israel out of Egyptian slavery. God had a plan! There are millions of young Black boys and young Black men who need saving from the fallacy of manhood so they can go on and fulfill the will of God in their lives, and in the lives of their families. Therefore, God is calling the Black woman into position to begin to bring to the forefront young Black men who are strong in character, morals, and intelligence, who love the Lord with all their heart.

The women who are candidates to become "The Strength of Black America" will not be considered simply on the condition that she is Black only. This woman will need to be completely committed to God in every area of her life. This woman may not be considered to be very wise by society. Any woman who will do the will of God today, ill respective of her color or nationality, may not be considered to be wise by society standards. She may be considered a fool by today's standards of what a woman should be, but in all actuality she will be a very wise woman in the eyes of God. Proverbs 4:1: "Every wise woman buildeth her house: but the foolish plucketh it down with her hands."

This woman will not just have a traditional religious experience; she will walk in relationship with God. Her experience will cause her to commune with God. She will love the Lord more than her husband, children, family, and friends. She will want to do all that God says for her to do in His Word, more than what traditional religion has taught and popular opinion dictates. She will not be perfect and will never achieve perfection, but she will be a woman of prayer, obedience, and submission to God.

This woman is not a weak person. She may be mistaken for the kind of woman some consider to be a doormat to be walked on. But she will not tolerate disrespect or ill treatment from her husband or her children. In the case where a husband may abuse his wife physically, sexually, verbally, or emotionally, she must consider leaving the home until the problem can be worked out. Traditional beliefs cause people to think that to be what God wants you to be you must be weak and willing to be walked on by others. I submit that living for the Lord is just the opposite. There are certain things that a person that is in right standing with the Lord will not tolerate. And the reason they will not tolerate those certain things is because God's Word will tell her how she is to be treated. Being in right relationship with God helps the individual know his or her individual self-worth.

I want you to imagine this woman who is considered to be The Strength of Black America. She is a woman who is poised, a woman of strength, a woman of honor, a woman of impeccable character, and a woman of beauty because her beauty is within. [Every woman can be beautiful no matter what her physical characteristics are if she is beautiful within.] She is a virtuous woman, the description of which can be found in the book of Proverbs, chapter 31:10,31. Here are just a few excerpts from the 21 verses from The Living Bible translation: "If you can find a virtuous woman, she is worth more than precious gems! Her husband can trust her, and she will richly satisfy his needs. She will not hinder him, but help him all her life." "She is energetic, a hard worker, and watches for bargains. She works far into the night!" "She's a woman of strength and dignity, and has no fear of old age. When she speaks, her words are wise, and kindness is the rule for everything she says."

"She watches carefully all that goes on throughout her household, and is never lazy. Her children stand and bless her; so does her husband." "He praises her with these words: 'There are many fine women in the world, but you are the best of them all!'" "Charm can be deceptive and beauty doesn't last, but a woman who fears and reverences God shall be greatly praised."

Children are very impressionable and will believe whatever their mother or parents teach them at early ages. If a mother such as the one described in the preceding paragraphs teaches her child the biblical truth about God, who He is and what He wants, that child will have a foundation that is worth more than money, fame, or notoriety could ever afford. This child will believe in the God of his mother, and he will believe in himself and nothing will be withheld from him. The children of this mother would be taught the truth without being biased about human nature and people of all walks of life.

They will be taught responsibility and the value of hard work and a job well done. They will be taught respect for all people, because the God of their mother is no respecter of persons. He sees all to be equal in His sight. They would be taught the value of a good education. The essence of what could be taught is endless, and the virtues of those things are priceless.

Far too long Black families have had to suffer because the woman has been so abused she could not fulfill her purpose. Abused by Black men who had no knowledge of what God's expectations were of them to have wives. Instead of loving and nurturing his wife as Christ did the church, he has depleted her of the will to be this kind of woman described in Proverbs. Not understanding his purpose to his wife and family, he abused them. "If you do not understand the purpose of a thing, abuse is inevitable." It does not matter how much a man loves his wife. He cannot cause her to become this kind of woman. But his love, respect, and good treatment of her will cause her to want to be this kind of woman, and she will seek God's help to become what He, "God," wants her to be.

Men and women as well as the church have grossly misrepresented the position of submission by the woman in the marriage relationship and at home, which has caused untold damage to marriages, children, and homes alike. When Theresa and I first married, I did not have a good understanding of submission by women at all. Even though I really never vocalized exactly how I was thinking and believing, it came across in my actions. I remember while working at a chemical refinery during shift work I told all the guys on shift that when I got married they would see a change in how I come to work. Of course while I was single, I was bringing brown bag specials to work for lunch. I told them that they would not see any more brown bags because I was marrying a Christian woman who would be submissive and cook for me every day.

Working on shift with seventeen other men, most of whom were not saved, I was trying to be a good witness for Jesus. After Theresa and I married, it seemed as though I went to work for at least two months with that same brown bag special. I made such a big deal before marrying that my wife would cook that the guys were just waiting to see what was going to happen. In good spirit they teased me every day. They could not wait till I walked in the plant to see that brown bag, then they laughed and laughed! Those guys were right to laugh at me; I was not right in my thinking about my expectations of my wife. I thought she was supposed take good care of me and we were going to show everyone how it was supposed to be in marriage.

It was a good awakening for me. I loved Theresa so much, and I did not even think to ask her if she could cook before we married. I come to realize she did not know how to at the time. Once I was preaching and shared that story, and the congregation just laughed and laughed. Theresa and I were preaching at this church, and she was to preach that very next Sunday. When she took the podium, she told the people how I shared that story the week before, then she said, "Now here is the rest of the story."

I had failed to remember to tell the people that she did learn how to cook not very long after we were married, and just how well she could cook now. So she got me back that next Sunday, and the congregation thought it was hilarious. So let me tell you, Sis. Theresa can burn y'all! If I did not tell you, she may write a sequel to this book just to tell you that I forgot to tell you again.

When the Black woman begins to assume her position of power and not weakness, she will begin producing strong young Black men and women with a dependency on God, armed with morality, dignity, intelligence, integrity, character and a sense of strong family background. The young man will seek to marry, love, and nourish his wife. And the young woman will marry and love and submit to her husband, and they both will begin the cycle unto the next generation. The Black people of America must come to realize this is our purpose. This is why God has brought us to America, hallelujah!!

I can just imagine the women who read this and say, "I could be just like that if my husband or my children would just act right." Let me quickly say that no one can live this way of his or her own accord. Yet it is possible for this kind of life to be lived, but it can only be done through the grace and help of Almighty God. For the woman who truly fears and reverences God, she will allow Him to live His life through her. And if by chance her husband and children are not calling her blessed and praising her, they will if she continues to be committed to God so He can do in her what she wants and needs to be done.

There is a question in the minds of many married women who are saved and know the Lord. They are married and their spouses are not saved, and they wonder: *How can I be submissive to a man who is not saved, or should I even try to be submissive to a man who's not saved?* This is one area where the church has failed to teach women who are married about submission. It is biblical for a woman who is saved and married to an unsaved man to be submissive to her husband, even though he is not saved!

Keep in mind that submission is not what most people think it is. Submission is not so much an action as it is an attitude. I have witnessed many women trying to be submissive by "doing" something. And while they are doing an act, they are angry. Submission says within oneself that I want to do this. Submission is not when it is convenient or results in a favorable situation; it is an attitude regarding the will of God.

Submission does not suggest in any way that a wife should do whatever her husband asks of her. In other words, if a husband who is not saved asks his wife to do something that is contrary to the will of God, she is not obligated to implement his request, nor should she do it. But any suggestion or request he may have that is not contrary to will of God, it is expected by God that she should be willing and implement it. To be in submission does not mean that the woman is under dictatorship. She should be able to discuss with her husband the decision he makes and his request, and what her feelings are about them and how it will affect the family. This is what God meant when He said that "It is not good that man should be alone: I will make him a help meet for him." Someone suitable for him on his intellectual level, not just to do whatever he says without communicating.

The reason why God says it should be done this way is found in the Bible in the book of 1 Peter 3:1,5, the Modern Language Version: "In a similar way you wives should be submissive to your own husbands, so that if any of them will not be persuaded by the message, they may without message be won over by the conduct of their wives as they observe your chaste and respectful behavior.

"Your adornment should not be outward, braided hair, putting on gold trinkets, or putting on robes; instead it should be the inner personality of the heart with the imperishable qualities of a gentle and quiet spirit, something of surpassing value in God's sight. For in this way holy women of the past, who fixed their hope on God, adorned themselves, submissive as they were to their own husbands."

Many Christian women battle with this and choose not to submit themselves to God according to His Word and consequently not submit to their husbands. And still they want the church to pray that their husbands get saved. What God says is if the husband does not want to hear the Word of God, he can and will be affected if the wife is committed to God first, then submitted to her husband.

Then the Holy Spirit will have an avenue by which to work through to bring conviction in the life of her husband. Her life-style will be the very thing the Holy Spirit will use to deal with his heart. But if the wife says, "I am not going to do that," then she may very well be a hindrance to her husband getting saved. Then he will not want to hear about the Lord or the church because of the actions of his wife, who professes to know the Lord.

I have spoken with many women who are married to an unsaved man. They were already married before they got saved, and they want to know what can they do. I open the Bible to this scripture and expound on it, and they say, "There is no way I am going to submit myself to this man." It is God's way of dealing with an unsaved husband. Some have even gotten angry at the notion of submitting. But for the woman who is to be "The Strength of Black America," she will do whatever God asks of her.

Whether one agrees with it or not, God has divine order in everything He does. The military works within the framework of chain of command, or modus operandi. Our United States government operates under certain protocol. The judicial systems of America do the same. According to the Word of God, He established all these powers to be. The marriage was the very first institution God established, so it should work within the framework of God's divine plan. Here is God's divine plan and order for the home, found in the book of 1 Corinthians 11:3: "But I would have you to know, that the head of every man is Christ; and the head of the woman is the man; and the head of Christ is God."

Can you imagine what would happen to the military if everyone did what he or she wanted to when they wanted to? Can you imagine what would happen to the United States government if every branch of government did what it wanted to on its own? Can you imagine what it would be like to have a judicial system without certain guidelines to abide by? When it comes to the home today, everyone is just about doing whatever they feel, not giving any attention to God's divine order. Jesus said, "A house divided against itself cannot stand." Is it any wonder why we have so many broken homes, divorces, and wrecked lives, and children almost destroyed?

If there is a Black woman or any woman who will say, "I will assume this role vacated by so many women," you will began to see unsaved husbands getting saved and the home strengthened again. You will began to see young men become men, and you will begin to see the family structure thrive once again. However, this position cannot be assumed on one's own willpower; there must be a dependency on God. He will give you the strength and wisdom to walk in this dynamic position that can only be filled with women whose hearts are totally given over to the Lord.

If it is your desire to surrender your whole heart to the Lord, I want to invite you to pray. I would ask that you sincerely consider what your desire is. Jesus said it this way: "Count the cost." What this means is that what you are willing to do is to give your will to Him. Not only in this area alone, but your whole heart to Him. After that, and only after you have done that, you are ready to pray and ask His help.

Here is a sample of what you can pray: **"Dear heavenly father, it is my desire to become a women such as this. But I have failed to become this way in my own life. I have made mistakes. I have sinned and I am sorry for the things I have done and the life I have lived. Would you please help me to become the woman you planned for me to be…**

I want to live for you now with all my heart, but I don't know how to do that. Will you help me? I confess that I have sinned and chose a life different from what you intended. I confess that my sins have caused me to be lost, and I need your help to find my way.

I believe that Jesus Christ is your Son; I believe He died for my sins. I believe that He rose from the dead and is alive today. I am asking you to have mercy on me, and forgive me of all my sins.

I ask that your Spirit would come into my heart and life and give me the strength to become your child. I surrender all that I am to you at this moment. I belong to you now. Help me to live each day for you that I might draw closer to you.

Thank you, Lord, for saving me and accepting me as your child. In Jesus' name I pray, Amen!

The following is a prayer that can be prayed for women who are already saved and know the Lord Jesus as their personal Savior.

Dear Heavenly Father, I come to you in the name of my Lord Jesus. I have come to realize that I have not been the kind of wife, mother, and woman that I am reading about. I cannot deny that your Spirit has dealt with me regarding these issues. I have ignored the nudging and convictions of your Spirit. For this I am sorry, and I repent.

I have come to realize that I cannot live this kind of life on my own accord, and I do not know how to do it now. I need your help!

You have helped me in many ways and in many areas in my life, and I believe you are able to help me now.

I want to be this kind of woman; you created me to be this kind of woman! Now your desire has become mine. I trust you to begin to live your life in this area through me. I believe that according to your word that in my weakness your strength is made perfect. Help me now I pray, in Jesus' name, Amen!

Eight

Single Parent Homes in the Black Community

I grew up without having a father and mother at home together. I was raised in a single parent home. I am so thankful to God that I was raised in the single parent home that I was, though. My mother did what I think to be a phenomenal job in raising seven children alone during a time when it was extremely difficult financially to do so. My mother had to catch the city bus to work every day regardless of the weather conditions. She was a maid and cleaned house and cared for the children of the people she worked for. It was very difficult to make ends meet, but she managed to do it. She did it in such a way that all of my brothers and sisters and I never knew that we were considered poor. Because my mother, who we all call Ma Dea, taught us how to be rich through having good family relationships and mutual respect, we were only poor because of a lack of money and material possessions.

In the times in which we live today, single parent homes are more the norm than the complete family unit. Divorce is at such an alarming rate that it seems to be dominating society. People are not willing to work through problems anymore. They tend to take what they perceive to be an easy way out. When a comparison is done with those who profess Christianity and those who do not, statistics show results that are staggering, to say the least. The divorce rate is at 64% in America today.

There are just as many if not more divorces among Christians as those who do not profess religious beliefs or preferences. In some cases, because of the fear of divorce, many people decide to live together without the benefit of legally marrying in an effort to see if the relationship will work before marrying. That will never be the true test to see if a relationship will work. First of all, the relationship is getting off to a faulty start, and you cannot build anything that will last on a faulty foundation. In many of these cases children are born, and when the relationship dissolves, the results are just the same as a divorce. Some children are born to single parents from promiscuous relationships. Some even choose not to marry or to live together but want to raise a child or children. Or even in the case when the spouse of one dies, single parent homes have increased at an enormous rate.

While it is not impossible to raise children as a single parent, it is extremely difficult to do so. In times past it was somewhat difficult to raise children alone, but it seems today that it is far more difficult than what used to be. With the rising cost of living and all the challenges that itself brings, its tough. The challenges are greater, and the results of a failed effort have far more devastating consequences.

Compounding the difficulty are laws prohibiting parents from physically disciplining their children. I am one who absolutely stands against any form of child abuse, and believes those who abuse children should be severely punished to the fullest extent of the law. But according to the Word of God, physical discipline should be carried out because of loving the child and not for punishment sake. The Bible teaches that if you do not discipline your child, you do not love your child. Proverbs 13:24 says, "He that spareth his rod hateth his son: but he that loveth him chaseneth him betimes." The word hateth does not mean to "hate" as we understand the word to mean. It means to not love enough to do something about the rebellion in the child.

I have been in grocery stores and witnessed children disobeying their parents to the point of hitting back at them in defiance to what they want them to do. This is an embarrassment to parents that children show this kind of disrespect. This is in most cases a result of lack of loving discipline administered at home. I have also seen in some cases where parents slap children in the face during times like this, which is in itself wrong and provokes the child to be rebellious. Loving discipline should be done in the privacy of the home; then when children come out into public with their parents, they will have the respect they deserve as parents. But this goes further than just good behavior in the supermarket. It builds character and respect for authority, which is grossly lacking in many of America's youth today.

This is a marvelous example of why I believe our founding fathers who drafted the Constitution did not intend for the law regarding separation of church and state to separate God and state. It should not be the state's or the government's responsibility to tell parents how to raise their children. At the same time, I certainly understand why the government felt the need to step in. Due to the ever-increasing number of child abuse cases, something had to be done. If the state were not separated from God in the sense of excluding Him in its affairs, it would be able to use God's instructions for the disciplining of children without the penalty of the law.

As a result of not being able to institute God's instructions for disciplining children, or in some cases an unwillingness to discipline children, our homes and schools are not functioning properly. Students threaten parents and teachers even to the point of their lives. Some parents and teachers are afraid of students "with good reasons." Children are not disciplined, so they have no respect for authority. Parents cannot discipline for fear of going to jail. Teachers cannot and will not discipline for fear of being sued or going to jail, or at worst, get injured or even killed in the process. And all the while we are still losing our children. I believe it is all a diabolical plan to sabotage God's will for raising children, and it is working against those parents who will obey the government rather than God.

Quoting again from the book *The Making of America*, on page 15 it says, "One of the most exciting stories in American history is the account of the man who tunneled back into the ancient past and was among the first to rediscover the remarkable formula which allowed the United States to become the first free nation in modern times, that man was Thomas Jefferson. As a matter of fact, it took the early

Americans 180 years (1607–1787) to put it all together, but when it finally settled into place, their formula (**The Constitution of the United States of America**) ignited the fires of freedom all over the world."

"Perhaps there is a tendency to take much of this for granted. However, **Thomas Jefferson and the Founding Fathers warned that their formula for freedom could be lost in a single generation.**" This is why I believe the disciplining of our children is extremely important. This is also why I believe the devil is behind the judicial system to make it illegal to discipline our children. Because of a lack of discipline we are losing our children. The Founding Father feared that all it would take is the loss of one generation, and America's freedoms would be in jeopardy. That is because our freedom given to us from the Constitution was originally discovered as God instructed the nation of Israel how to live. The following is how all it takes is one lost generation, and the erosion of our freedom begins.

From the book *The Making of America*, on page 10, Samuel Langdom, in a speech before the Massachusetts legislature in 1788, declared: "On the people, therefore, of the United States, it depends whether wise men or fools, good or bad men, shall govern.... Therefore, I will now lift up my voice and cry aloud to the people.... From year to year be careful in the choice of your representatives and the higher powers [offices] of government. Fix your eyes upon men of good understanding and known honesty; men of knowledge, improved by experience; men who fear God and hate covetousness; who love truth and righteousness, and sincerely wish for the public welfare.... Let not men opening irreligious and immoral become your legislators.... If the legislative body are corrupt, you will soon have bad men for counselors, corrupt judges, unqualified justices, and officers in every department who will dishonor their stations.... Never give countenance to turbulent men, who wish to distinguish themselves and rise to power by forming combinations and exciting insurrections against government.... I call upon you to support schools in your towns.... It is a debt you owe to your children."

I lift up my voice and cry aloud to America and Christians as an evangelist and a man of God! "We are dangerously close to loosing a generation of young people who know nothing of the God of America who so moved the Founding Fathers of our nation. A generation of young people who know nothing of discipline from a godly perspective, and respect for parents and others. It is high time we awake out of this state of placebo and pray before we will have brought on our Founding Fathers' greatest fears: the changing of our Constitution, which will ultimately take away the freedoms Americans are accustomed to.

Many years ago America's parents feared God more than they feared the government, although there was no law against disciplining children then. They raised children with good manners and a healthy respect for authority and elders and especially God. They pulled out the belt, strap, a piece of wood, or a switch and obeyed God when their children disobeyed them. Consequently, children were disciplined at home, so there was respect for parents first, then teachers, policemen, elderly folk, and for other community leaders. God created mankind, and He knows what it takes to help correct us when we go wrong.

It is extremely difficult to raise a child in today's society. I have watched several of the talk show programs when kids and their parents were the subject. It reduces me to tears to see what parents go through dealing with rebellion from their children. Women head up the majority of single parent homes, so I will address most of my statements to women. There will be statements I am sure that will apply to men who head single parents homes as well.

What used to be the traditional home setting was the father and mother were married and both present at home. Usually the man is the disciplinarian, meaning he was tough. The women tend to be more soft and easygoing, and this is good, because there needs to be a balance in the raising of children. Too much of anything is not good (the old cliché goes); fathers need to be tough but compassionate and loving, and take an active role in the lives of their children. But when there is father, and the woman does not assume the role of toughness and disciplinarian, it could spell real trouble for the children, especially young men.

Men and women generally fight over the roles I have just described. Men will generally say to their wives, "You are too soft on the children." Women will generally say, "You are too tough on the kids." Sometimes neither understands that both are necessary to balance the raising of the children. Can you imagine a couple who both are like drill sergeants to their kids? Or can you imagine a couple who both are so weak and soft as to never discipline their child at all? In either case there will be an imbalance in what is needed in the child's upbringing.

I have come to realize that men tend to be tougher on their sons than their daughters. I have come to this understanding by Theresa and me raising our children. Women have the tendency to be tougher on their daughters than their sons. Why is this? I believe it is because men know what it takes to raise young boys into a man; of course, because he is a man. Women who head up their homes must be very careful regarding this. Young men need to learn how to work and work hard, and stay with a task until it is completed.

Then he will learn the value of a job well done, and at the same time learn to stay with a job until it is completed. In this way he will learn to maintain employment to support his family when he gets married. Fathers want to see this in their sons, so they push for it. If a single woman as a parent is too soft on her son, there is a tendency for him not to have the character and work ethics he will need as a man.

And mothers know what it takes to raise young girls into women. So when the father gets tough, the son has a tendency to go to his mother for comfort. When the mother gets tough on the daughter, she runs to the father for comfort. That is because both are needed. The father will comfort his daughter because he does not understand why his wife is tough on the girl. But the wife knows she must be tough to teach her daughter to have womanly skills. And so it is with the man and his son.

But this presents another situation for the single mother. She will have to learn to be both. Being that women head the majority of single parent homes, this presents a real challenge. There are many young Black boys who desperately need the male role model in their lives. But in the case where there is no male role model, the mother must assume this role. Oh yes! It is extremely difficult to do, but if she fails to do it, the young man will grow up without the propensity to develop into a man, as he should. She may in turn pamper him, instead of doing the accepted thing to help him to become a man.

Women need to be especially careful with their daughters also. Many women deep within their hearts resent the way their mothers raised them, not understanding that their mothers were trying to help them to become a woman with womanly skills. Many of the older women perhaps resented the way their mothers raised them, so the resentment has been passed down. So many women say they do not want to be like their mothers because they picked up the resentment that was in them. In Ezekiel 16:44, the prophet said this about women, "As is the mother, so is the daughter." If today's mother is not careful, she will repeat what her mother did with her with her own daughter. It may not be her desire to become like her mother, but more than likely she will. She must be careful to guard against resentment.

I would like to use my own mother as an example as to how she raised seven children alone after her marriage was dissolved. She had to be the father and mother, and she accepted that role and responsibility. I am the youngest of the seven. I had four sisters (we lost one of my sisters unfortunately to cancer, and we all miss her dearly) and two older brothers. I would hate to think what would have become of us if my mother had not taken the role of the disciplinarian she did in our home. She had to be both the father and mother. We were raised in and around a neighborhood that afforded each of us with many opportunities to get involved in many things that were not good.

My mother believed that if you spare the rod you spoil the child. She would ask the questions, who? what? where? why? when? I would be on the phone later than what she told me to be, trying to be cool with the girls, Ma Dea would pick up the phone, and the conversation and my coolness would come to an abrupt end. If grades were not good she would get on to us. She had a vision, and she was determined that she would see it come to pass, that all of her seven children would at least graduate from high school. Her dream came to pass and completion after I graduated.

I remember my oldest brother came home once with a jacket and knife belonging to a gang he had joined. This was around the year 1959 or 1960 or so. I remember my mother telling him to take them back and get out of the gang, or find somewhere else to live. He got out and never looked back. She would make each of us clean up every day before we left the house to play or do anything else. She had her boys clean the commode as well as wash the dishes, things that some young men were taught to be woman's work. My mother used to say if your wife ever gets sick, you need to know how to take care of her. And you know what? Today I can do just that! This was because of how my mother being a single parent trained us.

During the time I was twenty or twenty-one years old, I would keep very late hours, coming in during the wee hours of the morning. Ma Dea told me once that if I came in another night at 2 A.M., I could just find somewhere else to spend the night. I would be at a pool hall and lose track of time. I remember coming in one morning after 2 A.M. and the door was locked. I knocked as usual but there was no answer. She never came to the door, so I slept in the car out in the yard. I never did that again. She would always tell us "as long as you are living in my home you will obey me." Well, each of us tested her, but she never backed down.

I remember her telling me that "if you ever got into trouble with the police for something you had done wrong, do not call me to get you out of trouble." Well, I did exactly what she told me not to do. When I was around twenty years old, I spent a night in jail on a misdemeanor charge. I was so scared because I had never been in trouble before, so I called my mother. She asked me, "Did you do it?" Then she said to me, "I told you if you got into trouble for something you did, do not call me to get you out." It brought reality to me, and I learned responsibility for my actions that night. I had money in my pocket that night to bond out of jail, but never having any experience with the judicial system, I stayed the night in jail and got out the next morning. It turned out to be the best lesson I ever learned, thanks to my mother. I must have aged at least five years during that one night.

I remember thinking how mean that was of my mother to do that. But after having my own children, I later realized how it must have torn her heart apart to tell me that. I came to realize that she could not have slept a wink that night because her youngest child was in jail. She never had a child in jail before that, even though it was just one night. She did what she did because she loved me. Judge the results; I have never been in trouble with the police or judicial system since.

I have seen many parents bail their children out of trouble on simple things, and later they went on to greater crime because they felt like their parents would bail them out every time. I know of situations where parents have sold all they have and put up their homes for collateral to bail their children out of trouble. I thank God for a mother who had it in her to be tough when she needed to be. Incidentally, none of my brothers or sisters ever had any trouble with the police or anything else. It was all due to our mother taking on the role of an absent male role model. Praise God!

I used to think my mother was so mean, because she used to whip me all the time. There where times when she would whip all of us at the same time if we were disobedient to her. I thought the youngest child was supposed to be spoiled and get their way. My mother had other ideas. She was determined I was not going to be spoiled. Oh, how I thank God every day for what she did. It was not until I accepted the Lord in my life when I was twenty-three years old that I realized the importance of what she did. I sat down and wrote her a letter with tears in my eyes saying thank you for whipping me the way you did. You see, the way I was, had she not taken the initiative to not spare the rod, I would have been gone. I was one of those children who would dare anything. It is safe for me to say I would not even be here today had it not been for my mother taking on this responsibility.

Today's parents cannot afford to be weak or afraid! When I would view the talk shows on television, one thing was quite evident. The parents of those kids were scared of their own children. I want to say something that might be a little tough, but I believe it needs to be said. "Children are not all the blame for where they are today. The majority of the blame falls on the parents." I understand that even in some cases where parents did all the right things, children still can go wrong. But there are not nearly enough parents today who are willing to discipline their children in love and take charge in their homes.

I often hear parents say that children do not come with instructions. Well, I do not exactly agree with that statement. The Bible teaches that children are a heritage of the Lord. It says in Psalms 127:3: "Lo, children are an heritage of the Lord: and the fruit of the womb is his reward." God has loaned us our children so we can raise them to know and seek after Him. He gave instructions as to how to do just that. Our problem is we have not applied what He said for us to do. We refuse to accept God's ways for the proper raising of our children. We tend to believe that to discipline children is too tough. But I want you to hear what the Lord himself says.

The following Scripture verses are taken from the *Living Bible* version for easier understanding. Proverbs 13:24: "If you refuse to discipline your son, it proves you don't love him; for if you love him you will be prompt to punish him." Proverbs 19:18: "Discipline your son in his early years while there is hope. If you don't you will ruin his life." Proverbs 22:15: "A youngster's heart is filled with rebellion, but punishment will drive it out of him." Proverbs 23:13: "Don't fail to correct your children; discipline won't hurt them! They won't die if you use a stick on them! Punishment will keep them out of hell." Proverbs 22:15: "Foolishness is bound in the heart of a child; but the rod of correction shall drive it far from him."

Because of these truths our judicial system has been manipulated by the devil into making it against the law to physically discipline children. Please allow me to explain. Not very many people know and understand that there is a literal devil. And that he can and will work within our judicial system to change laws to suit his purpose. The law making it unlawful to discipline children the way God said was done on the back of protecting children from abuse. The issue of protecting children from abuse certainly needed to be addressed, but I think the phrase "throwing the baby out with the bath water" applies here. Making it illegal to discipline children has not stopped child abuse, but it has in far to many cases stopped good child development. Parents are afraid of their children calling 911, but if you discipline your children while they are very young, they will have too much respect for you to call 911 as they get older.

This is what the devil wanted to happen, because he wants to have inroads to our children, and rebellion is his way to get to them. Ultimately, we could lose a generation of young people and lose the freedoms we currently have in this country. The Bible says rebellion is in the heart of a child. That is because all children were born that way because of Adam and Eve's transgression. If this rebellion is left intact in the heart of the child, it will flourish into outright rebellion against society. Proverbs 29:15 in the *Living Bible* says, "Scolding and spanking a child helps him to learn. Left to himself, he brings shame to his mother." If rebellion is not met with discipline, eventually the child will give in to it.

More and more in society today, people are marrying into relationships where children are already present. In today's time it is almost rare to see two single people marry having no children involved. This presents additional challenges in the lives of the children involved. It is a very delicate situation that should be approached with extreme caution. Marriage in itself is quite a challenge when no children are involved. To complicate the situation is to marry unprepared for this two-fold challenge. For the woman who has children and wants to marry, she should really undergo intense scrutiny of the man she is willing to marry.

Too many cases have occurred where women have married only to find out that the person she married was not the person for her children. This has a tremendous psychological and emotional effect on both the mother and the children. I believe it is safe for me to say, based on my experience with many Black men, that marring a woman with children belonging to another man has challenges the woman knows nothing of. Deeply rooted in the heart of most Black men is the thought that he does not want to take care of another man's child or children. It has been deeply rooted in him by older Black men who knew no better than to endanger the well-being of children who do not have their biological fathers to raise them, by putting this foolish thought in the minds of young Black men, who will eventually marry women with children.

Even though the man may very well be in love with the mother, it will take some time for him to build the proper relationship with her child or children. The mother must be willing to let the man go if he is not right for the children. The truth is he is not just marring a wife; he is inheriting a family.

On the other hand, the woman must be willing to allow her new husband rights to be the child's or children's father. It is clearly understood that he can never be the biological father, but he must have freedom to be the father of the children whose mother he married. Women, if you are not willing to relinquish some control to your new husband, you are not ready for marriage with children involved. The children should be made aware that a new person is entering their lives. Not just as Momma's new husband, but also a father and an authority figure with Momma. If the children are going to be developed properly, this must be established. Too many children are growing up with father figures who have little or no relationship with them, resulting in a child having no relationship with a male authority figure in the home that they respect. It is a complicated situation in more ways, because in some cases biological fathers are still involved in their children's lives.

There have been men in this situation who are very eager to discipline children who are not their own biologically. "If disciplining a child brings you no pain, then you are the wrong person to discipline." I have helped to raise two children who were not mine biologically. I must confess that at the beginning of my marriage, I began disciplining my two children when there was no pain in it for me. I believe children know when you are disciplining them in love, and they know when you do not feel pain, or when you do it in anger.

We should never discipline in anger whether we are biological parents are not. But it comes easier to discipline without feelings if you are not the biological parent. Whenever I did that, I would feel real guilty that I did. I tried to cover it up with statements such as "they needed the discipline." And they may have needed it, but I do not think it was the right time for me to have performed it.

You see, I used to be one to say I would never marry a woman with another man's children. It was deeply rooted in me also. But when I came to know the Lord, my whole outlook on life changed. But my thinking had to catch up with my heart. So not only was I feeling guilty, the Holy Spirit began convicting me. Then I began to concentrate on them and their feelings as well as mine, and it began to happen. It began to hurt me when I would administer discipline. I wish I could say I did everything right, but unfortunately that's just not the case, but I have learned a few good things.

The common term used in this kind of situation is "stepparents, and stepchildren." It should never once come out of the mouth of either parent. And the children should be taught not to use the term. I can at least say I have been married for twenty years, and the term never came out of my mouth, nor have I ever thought it, and it has never been used in our family. I believe when the term is used, it will always keep distance between that parent and the children.

It is extremely difficult for women who are single with children. My hat is off to them. It is also very tough on women who are married with children. In fact, it is very difficult to be a woman, I suppose. Women who are single with children have the full load and responsibility of the children; and as well, women who are married have the same responsibility. Women who are married and have to work should have the help of their husbands in every area of the family home. She has the full-time responsibility of a job and should have part-time responsibility with the children and the household responsibilities if she works.

In many cases, because of economics, it is necessary that the woman work, but in those cases where it is not necessary, it would be wise for the woman not to work. This, of course, is predicated on the idea that she has children. Children are a full-time responsibility if the woman works or not. In the event where the woman does not have to work, she still should not have the full responsibility of the children, or her household responsibilities. Her husband should also help with both. Career-minded women should not plan to have children until they fulfill their desire to accomplish their goal. I say this because children need their mothers much more than a career-minded woman is able to give herself to them. I am conscience of the fact that sometimes women get pregnant before the time they plan.

I am in no way trying to dictate what an individual should do with their life, but if you are going to have children, you should at least plan their lives as well as your own. I understand that in the times in which we live, women hold positions that are very stressful, time-consuming, and demanding. Ten to twelve hour days are not suitable for women with children. A woman would have to be Superwoman to raise children when she works; I wonder how it is possible with the responsible positions women hold today. Many women who work are somewhat critical of women who do not work.

They tend to think that all they do all day is lie around the house, watch television, and do nothing. It is my contention that mothers who stay home with their children work much harder than women who actually leave the house to go to work, if they raise their children properly, that is! I have watched my wife raise our children, and it is far more work involved than what most people think. I used to hear other women remark to my wife that she should be able to do many things because she does not work. Well, after having witnessed it firsthand, it is no small task. Some of the statements had sarcasm in them, and they would affect my wife's feelings many times.

Single woman have it far more difficult when it comes to raising children. I cannot imagine having to do what these women have to do. But I must say this responsibility comes with having children. I know that not very many women agree with what I am saying. My next statement will have to be understood spiritually to make sense. Women have had to work extremely hard to get where they are today. And on the surface it looks very good, but take a good look around America today and see our children. They are the forgotten generation, left behind in the pursuit of gaining independence, economic status, and chasing dreams.

I believe this is a diabolical plan of the devil to rob us of a generation of young people, and we are all responsible for it, men and women alike. I understand and believe that men have inflicted enormous pain and suffering on women to cause them to want to seek their independence and rights. And I believe that women should have both, but not at the risk of losing generations of kids who do not know their parents. Or the parents they do know are too stressed out to be good parents.

What is needed here? I believe what is needed is what God said to the people of Israel when they got into much trouble in their lives. The Lord spoke to Solomon after he had built the temple for the Lord and offered prayer for the people of God. God said these words: "I have heard thy prayer, and have chosen this place to myself for an house of sacrifice. If I shut up the heaven that there be no rain, or if I command the locust to devour the land, or if I send pestilence among my people; If my people, which are called by my name, shall humble themselves, and pray, and seek my face, and turn from their wicked ways; then will I hear from heaven, and will forgive their sin, and will heal their land."

That is exactly what we as a people need to do today. It's called "REPENT." It is not a very popular term today. But it still gets God's attention, and it is the answer to our dilemma.

Nine

It's Time Black America Awaken, God Is Calling!

God is calling! What a profound thought! Do you remember when God called to Moses out of the burning bush, saying "Moses, Moses?" And he said, "Here am I." And He said, "Draw nigh hither: put off thy shoes from off thy feet, for the place whereon thou standest is holy ground." Moses would never be the same after that experience. Do you remember when God called Samuel? Eli the priest told him to answer by saying "Speak, Lord; for thy servant heareth." And the Lord said to Samuel, "Behold, I will do a thing in Israel, at which both the ears of every one that heareth it shall tingle." Samuel would never be the same.

The Lord through the apostle Paul was calling out to the church at Rome to awaken out of sleep. Paul wrote to Rome to advise them to awaken from sleep, that knowing the time, it was the dawning of a new day. Here's the account of this in Romans 13:11,14: "And that, knowing the time, that now it is high time to awake out of sleep: for now is our salvation nearer than when we believed. The night is far spent, the day is at hand: let us therefore cast off the works of darkness, and let us put on the armour of light. Let us walk honestly, as in the day; not in rioting and drunkenness, not in chambering and wantonness, not in strife and envying. But put ye on the Lord Jesus Christ, and make not provision for the flesh, to fulfill the lust thereof." The apostle used the term *high time* to awake out of sleep. High time means "the right time, suitable or convenient time; the opportune point of time at which a thing should be done." He also used the term *to awake*. It means "the collecting of ones faculties: to awaken; rouse from sleeping, from sitting or lying, from obscurity, inactivity, non-existence." Another term used was *out of sleep*, meaning "spiritual torpor; torpor means extreme sluggishness, stagnation of function, apathy or dullness."

In a similar way, the message the apostle Paul had written to the Roman Church can be adopted and given to the Blacks of America today. It is high time to awaken out of sleep, God is calling! The dawning of a new day is occurring. This is the opportune time to awaken. God is moving among the Black people in American like never before. It is time to awaken out of spiritual torpor, extreme sluggishness, stagnation, and apathy about the things of God and about ourselves.

Apathy has been Black America's demeanor concerning the truth of God's Word. I believe we have been hungry for something for so long, and we have tried to satisfy this hunger with everything but truly coming to the Lord with all our heart. Now God is sending a clarion call. He is not just calling Blacks, but all men. God is not willing that any should perish, but that all might come to repentance and the saving knowledge of His Son Jesus Christ.

America as it stands today has turned her back on God. The Word of God says, "Righteousness exalts a nation, but sin is a reproach to any people." Our government, Congress, the Senate, the Supreme Court of the United States, and a host of churches have just about completely turned their backs on God. America makes a clear and distinct resonance that it does not want God's principles of morality governing society today.

I think that most Americans can clearly see that something is going on with our government and its lack of allegiance to God. The statement that many churches have turned their backs to God may have caused some thought of inquiry. But the truth is, far more churches than we want to believe do not want the principles of God as their foundations anymore, or the Word of God governing their actions. We have churches ordaining homosexuals to preach. This one act alone contradicts actions God has taken against the spirit of homosexuality in Sodom and Gomorrah. Some churches sanction same-sex marriages. God never intended for two women or two men to marry of the same sex.

When God first created man, he made a man and a woman and called them man and wife. God never makes a mistake; He did not create a man in a woman's body, or a woman in a man's body. Any church or nation that accepts the sin of homosexuality as an acceptable alternate life-style does not want God governing their actions. Many of our churches have adopted secular humanism over the Word of God; instead of teaching the truth of God's Word, we teach what man has conjured up and believe to be truth. Most churches have compromised their beliefs and given in to the pressure of being politically correct. It is politically correct to accept the life-style of homosexuals as an acceptable alternate life-style. It may be politically correct, but it is morally wrong.

God says in Romans 1:21-22: "Because that, when they knew God, they glorified him not as God, neither were thankful; but became vain in their imagination, and their foolish heart was darkened. Professing themselves to be wise, they became fools." Romans 1:24, 28 goes on to to say, "Wherefore God also gave them up to uncleanness through the lust of their own hearts, to dishonour their own bodies between themselves: Who changed the truth of God into a lie, and worshipped and served the creature more than the Creator, who is blessed forever. Amen. For this cause God gave them up unto vile affections: for even their women did change the natural use into that which is against nature:

"And likewise also the men, leaving the natural use of the woman, burned in their lust one toward another; men with men working that which is unseemly, and receiving in themselves that recompence of their error which was meet. And even as they did not like to retain God in their knowledge, God gave them over to a reprobate mind, to do those things which are not convenient."

Americans see all the problems we are having today as opposed to what America used to have. Everyone everywhere is trying to figure out what has gone wrong! The answer is basically simple: we have gone our own way away from God. Look what the prophet Isaiah had to say in Isaiah 1:2,4: "Hear, O heavens, and give ear, O earth: for the Lord hath spoken, I have nourished and brought up children, and they have rebelled against me. The ox knoweth his owner, and the ass his master's crib: but Israel doth not know, my people doth not consider. Ah sinful nation, a people laden with iniquity, a seed of evildoers, children that are corrupters: they have forsaken the Lord, they have provoked the Holy One of Israel unto anger, they are gone away backward."

America has basically done the same thing. Our history is rich with the bountiful blessings of God. We sing about it in our songs about America, "America! America! God shed his grace on thee." Since the most horrific event perhaps in the history of our country, which occurred on September 11, 2001, when highjacked airplanes flew into the Trade Center Towers in New York, I see signs and bumper stickers everywhere saying "God Bless America."

God has already blessed America. It is time for America to once again turn toward God and bless Him! When we as a nation began to embrace that which God is opposed to, we push God out of our affairs. Look what happens when we do that; He has been pushed out of our schools, and what happens? We have pushed Him out of our government, and look what happens. We have pushed Him out of our churches, and look what happens. Now we are pushing Him out of society. Is it any doubt why something like September 11, 2001, can happen to the once most powerful nation in the world?

God is putting out a clarion call to Black people. A people who have been in a spiritual torpor, because of not having the truth as a foundation to work from. A people who have been abused and have managed to come through it. A people who have been touched with compassion for the hardship of others. A people scorned by society. But this is just like God to do this. Why? Because this is this kind of people that God uses best. It was said of Abraham Lincoln that the reason he was sympathetic to the problems and plight of slaves was because he suffered in his early life and could identify with the suffering of others.

Listen to what God says about the type of people He chooses to use. In the book of 1 Corinthians 1:27-28 it says, "But God hath chosen the foolish things of the world to confound the wise; and God hath chosen the weak things of the world to confound the things which are mighty; And base things of the world, and things which are despised, hath God chosen, yea, and things which are not, to bring to nought things that are: That no flesh should glory in His presence." I saw a sign on a Baptist church just the other day that read like this, "God doesn't call the qualified, He qualifies the called."

God is now looking toward Black people once again. I use the term once again because by Moses He came to the Black man before once long, long ago. In the book of Numbers, chapter 10, after Moses and the children of Israel were freed from Egyptian bondage and ready to start their journey toward the Promised Land, Moses came to his brother-in-law named Hobab (Moses was married to a Black woman). His brother-in-law was the son of Raguel the Midianite, a Black man.

Moses asked for his help, and here is what it says in Numbers 10:29,32: "And Moses said unto Hobab, the son of Raguel the Medianite, Moses' father-in-law, We are journeying unto the place of which the Lord said, I will give it you: come thou with us, and we will do thee good: for the Lord hath spoken good concerning Israel. And he said unto him, I will not go; but I will depart to mine own land, and to my kindred. And he said, leave us not, I pray thee; forasmuch as thou knowest how we are to encamp in the wilderness, and thou mayest be to us instead of eyes. And it shall be, if thou go with us, yea, it shall be, that what goodness the Lord shall do unto us, the same will we do unto thee."

The Promised Land was not heaven. It was, however, a place that would have everything Israel would ever need. The Lord told Moses it was a land flowing with milk and honey. Moses told his brother-in-law, "If you come with us we will do thee good," because God had said how He would bless Israel, and in turn they would bless Him. Hobab said to Moses that he would not go, that he would return to his own land and to his people. Moses pleaded with Hobab not to leave them, because Hobab knew how to encamp in the wilderness. He knew how to make it through the rough places.

The wilderness was a very rough place, and Moses did not know how to make it through the rough places. Hobab was experienced in making it through the wilderness in rough places, so Moses pleaded with him not to leave them. Moses said to Hobab that he would be to them instead of eyes. This meant that even though they could see with their normal vision, Hobab had experience that was beyond just seeing with normal vision, because he had been through rough places many times before. He would be to them as a guide to lead the way in the forefront position. Not because of his color, but because of his experience in going through very difficult situations.

Please allow me to portray an analogy and parallel here with this truth, and Blacks today. America today is in perhaps some of the most difficult times ever. America has had some extremely difficult times in our past, but the circumstances of those times were different from what we are experiencing today. I am much too young to have experienced the time of the Depression in America, but I understand that it was a devastating time in our country. That was an economic problem and could be overcome by the working of money, something that Black Americans could not be of any help with. But where we are today, money cannot solve the problems facing our homes and families in America.

Even people who may be rich monetarily are in deep trouble today. The kinds of problems Americans are facing today cannot be solved with money. Even most of our churches are without answers for their parishioners. I think we are beginning to find out that secular humanism, psychology, psychic reading, horoscopes, etc., are not working. Americans are losing their children today to things money cannot satisfy. Moral decency has been lost, and people are feeling as though they have no self-worth anymore. Probably because their self-worth was all based upon what they have or do not have.

God is calling on a people who have some resiliency that have gone through rough times and know how to make it. A strong people who have learned to survive, even though they felt as though they had no self-worth. Blacks have undergone some extraordinary times and have had some experience with having resilience. They know how to make it through rough places and rough times.

Black Americans, however, must answer the call of God before they can be of any help to anyone. God will never use people or individuals who are totally dependent on their experiences and abilities.

That is why the Scripture says in Romans "that no flesh should glory in His presence." But for the people who have been tested and come through trusting God, they will become a mighty tool in the hand of the Almighty God who is able to do the miraculous.

Black America must awaken out of sleep at the call of God. It is high time to stop meandering around doing nothing. He who has called us to America has been with us even though we have not sought for Him. He wants us to know that Blacks have not made it on their own will. Now He is calling Blacks to awaken from a spiritual torpor and to come to God that He might use us for His purpose in our personal lives and in America.

Ten

It's Time for the
Prodigal to Come Home

The blessedness of coming home! Can you ponder the thought of going home? The famous words spoken by the character Dorothy on *The Wizard of Oz* "there's no place like home" have such meaning. It makes no difference where you are in life, and many are far better off than when they left home; there is still no place that can equal to home. Home is not necessarily a geographical location, though in some cases it can be. Home is where all of your worries tend to disappear. There is a feeling of peace, safety, comfort, and tranquility. The pressures of life tend to disappear. Sometimes life's challenges get to be so tough I revert back to when I was a child at my mother's home with no pressure, stress, or worry, and for a fleeting moment peace comes. Then an overwhelming desire takes me over to want to go back home.

In chapter 15 of the book of Luke in the Word of God, it tells of a parable about a father raising two sons. The youngest son decided he wanted to leave home and live a life apart from the way his father had raised him. The young man asked his father for his portion of the inheritance that his father would leave to his family in the event of his death. The young man took the portion of the inheritance that was given to him and went into a far country and spent it foolishly. Jesus called this young man a prodigal, one who did not want to live by his father's principles and decided to separate himself from his father and go his own way.

Jesus said the prodigal spent his inheritance wastefully; of course, he was referring to money. The prodigal whom I wish to reveal in this chapter has not spent money wastefully, but has spent his life wastefully. He spent his mind, his time, his abilities, his strength, his love, his youth and old age wastefully. The prodigal whom I am referring to is the Black people of America. Black people have been graced with all the same abilities as any other human being, in many cases even greater ability.

The sixteenth President of the United States of America, Abraham Lincoln, declared in his Gettysburg address in 1863: "Four score and seven years ago, our fathers brought forth on this continent, a new nation, conceived in Liberty, and dedicated to the proposition that all men are created equal." Black men and women are created the same as any other race of people, no more no less.

During the early years of our great nation, Blacks were not considered to be equal to White people. Blacks and all people were taught that White men were superior to the Blacks, so, in turn, Black children were raised thinking that somehow they were different and inferior to the White man. The God-given abilities to use their minds were never tapped into, and they were never trained to believe that they were just as able as any man to use his ability to think. What a travesty! "A mind is a terrible thing to waste." So the Black man wasted this God-given ability on things that were not important.

When I was a child in school studying American History, whenever Blacks made significant achievements in the field of education or science it would be played down or not accredited publicly. Credit would be given to others in the same field. I remember great accomplishments by Black athletes, singers, or dancers. But anything relating to using their minds was not accredited.

So the Black man has been, and, to some degree today, still is a prodigal in the sense of wasting his God-given abilities and talents. He is still a prodigal in the truest since of being away from his Father, God. The parable Jesus told was a natural illustration of a spiritual point He was making. The Father in the parable represented God, and the prodigal was away from his father, who was God. So the Black man today is still a prodigal if he is still away from God.

In the book of Luke, chapter 15:17, Jesus said of the prodigal that he came to himself. After squandering his inheritance on what Jesus called "riotous living," he spent all that he had. Then there came a famine in the land. He literally found himself in the "hog pin." He was eating what the swine was eating, and then the Scripture said, "He came to himself." Trouble has a way of causing you to look at yourself in a way that you do not when things are going well. I guess another way of saying it is "he came to his senses."

I believe that we are quickly embarking on an hour when God by the Holy Spirit will cause the Black Man to come to himself. This is a most dreadful experience and yet is a most liberating experience at the same time. Dreadful because he reaches a point in his life where he realizes that his life is not going anywhere. This is a time when an individual reaches a point when they realize that they have failed to obtain happiness, success, fame, fortune, etc. You realize that you have made a mess of your life. Even if certain things were attained, peace of mind and peace with God have not been obtained. It is liberating because then and only then God can really do what He wants to do in that individual's life.

I can vividly remember the day when by the help and grace of Almighty God I came to myself. This experience happened just prior to my salvation experience. My life was getting progressively worse; sin was dragging me into a downward spiral. I had been for most of my life at that time a clean-cut athlete all throughout high school. I had always been in great physical condition from training. After starting college on an athletic scholarship, I began to get involved in things that began to carry me down. Mainly drugs, marihuana, then on to a few other drugs, and I was sinking fast. I would never do anything like that in high school, but the peer pressure seemed to be greater at college.

Eventually I could no longer sustain myself. I had lost all interest in school and in the sport of baseball, which I loved more than anything. I made a terrible decision and walked away from a college education and a shot at playing professional baseball. A few years later, at the age of twenty-three, I cannot exactly remember the month or the date, but I remember the experience. I will never forget it. I remember one morning after a night of partying I arose and went to my bathroom. While washing my face and brushing my teeth, I began to stare at myself. It was an unusual stare. It was as though I was looking not only at my physical appearance but also at my whole life, and into my soul.

I just stood in front of that mirror and looked until I began to cry at what I was seeing. It was the kind of look that only God can allow you to execute. I began to feel so terrible, as I was only able to stare. I was accustomed to seeing a healthy physical specimen of a young man. But what I was seeing was anything but that! Sin has a way of blinding you to yourself. I felt so terrible and knew I needed help to change my life. But I had no inkling of how to began to do that. I was going over my life, the opportunities I had missed, the bad decisions I had made, and the things I was involved in. I remember breaking and weeping profusely and thereby "coming to myself."

I would later come to realize that this was the process that began my homecoming unto the Lord. This prodigal was on his way home. It felt terrible to look at myself for what I really was. But by the grace of God, He brought me to that point. Within a very short period of time after that experience, I made it home to my heavenly Father. Within a couple of weeks after that experience, I had the experience that would ultimately bring me to God. I was on my way to New Orleans for a weekend of gambling. I was playing pool to make money.

It was a Friday evening, and I was on Interstate 10 East heading toward New Orleans, which was only an eighty-six-mile drive. As I was driving alone in my car, all of a sudden I felt a presence in my car. I do not know how I knew it was the presence of the Lord, but I was acutely aware of His presence. I began to cry out and ask the Lord to forgive me for everything I had done. I was so under conviction I tried to remember each sin one by one to ask Him to forgive me, until I realized I could not remember them all and just asked Him to have mercy on me.

All of a sudden I felt this tremendous peace and sense of serenity come over me. I felt like someone had taken an enormous load off me. I experienced a joy that I had never known before. I felt strangely different from within, unlike anything I had ever experienced. At that time I had substance in my car that was illegal. I had the courage and state of mind to roll down my window and throw it all out on the interstate. I took a pack of cigarettes out of my pocket and tossed them also. I was so changed, so different, I felt brand new.

I did not gamble that night, I did not drink that night, and I did not smoke that night. It was the beginning of a brand-new life for me. My friends wondered what had happened to me! When I returned home no one understood what had happened to me. I'm sure many of my friends and some of my family thought I had lost it mentally. This was twenty-four years ago as I write, and I am still experiencing His presence in a profound way. As I looked back on these events after a few years, I could see how the Lord brought me there. You know hindsight is perfect. My awareness of the process began when I looked in that mirror in my bathroom that morning. I will never forget the experience of coming to myself.

God is moving and trying to bring Black people to themselves, whereas we will take a good look and come to the realization that our problem is not what we have believed all these years. We are going to begin to look and say, "I am sick and tired of myself." This will be the beginning of the awakening. This process has already begun with thousands of Blacks in America. In the parable Jesus tells what the father did when he saw his son coming home from a great distance. In Luke 15:20, He said, "But when he was yet a great way off, his father saw him, and had compassion, and ran, and fell on his neck, and kissed him." Love and forgiveness were not an issue with the father in this parable who was representative of God. There is an old saying in the Black community: "If you make one step toward God, He'll make two toward you." He's waiting for you!

If Blacks ever refuse the leading of the Holy Spirit by the Lord to come to themselves, they will never be able to really come home to the Father God. You see, this process of coming to yourself is not within the ability of man to do himself. God by His Holy Spirit is the only way to accomplish this in a human being. Jesus said of Himself in St. John 14:6, "I am the way, the Truth, and the Life: no man cometh unto the Father but by me." Then in St. John 6:44, Jesus said, "No man can come to me, except the Father which hath sent me draw him." St. John

3:16 says, "For God so loved the world, that he gave His only begotten Son." It is because of God's love for us that he by His Spirit draws us to the saving Knowledge of his Son Jesus. That is why Jesus says no one can come to Him unless God draws him.

The drawing Jesus is referring to is when the Holy Spirit begins to deal with an individual's heart and life. Sometimes He sends people to you. Other times He speaks through different means, bringing one as he did the prodigal "to himself." The truth is man never chooses to come to God. It cannot be done that way, and here is what Jesus said St. John 15:16: "Ye have not chosen me, but I have chosen you." It is an established fact in the Word of God that men do not come to God on their own, of their own accord. The prodigal came back to the Father because of the Holy Spirit dealings with him. I came to the Father because of the dealings of the Holy Spirit. Every man, woman, boy, or girl who ever comes to the Lord comes because they were prodded by the Holy Spirit; because God loves man so much.

The Holy Spirit in these last days is dealing with all human beings, trying to bring them "to themselves." As long as people say within them, "I'm okay" or "I'm not all that bad," or measure themselves by judging what others do or don't do, this journey home to the Lord will not happen. Without this journey home to the Father, human life is so incomplete. It does not matter how successful one's life may appear to be. It does not matter how rich in material things one might have. It does not matter what your race or nationality is. Without God in your life you are incomplete.

God created life in every individual. It is impossible for life to be fulfilled without Him who gave life. Those who manage to obtain some success in life apart from God, or try to find fulfillment in other things or other people, only find that they are void of something. That something is God He created us for Himself, and nothing will ever be able to fill that void but Him. Only Jesus Christ can slake the thirst of the human soul.

Those who will allow the Holy Spirit to bring them to that place of coming to themselves, will find themselves taking the first step on that wonderful road home to their Father who waits for them. They will become so fulfilled in life, even if they have never accomplished anything as far as success in society is concerned. For the one who has managed to be successful will finally come to the realization that they never experienced the joy of their success as much as their homecoming to the Father God. What an exciting time to be alive!

Even while some of you are reading this book, the Lord has been dealing with your heart, and you are in the place where this process is beginning. Remember this very important point that Jesus said in the parable about the prodigal when he came to himself. He said, "I will arise and go to my father, and will say unto him, Father, I have sinned against heaven and before thee."

Before the prodigal can come home after finally coming to himself by the help of the Holy Spirit and by the grace of God, he will need to recognize that he has sinned against heaven and against God. After he comes to himself in this way, he will realize he has sinned and will come home to the Father who is waiting to run to him and fall on his neck and say, "For this my son was dead, and is alive again; he was lost and is found" (Luke 15:24). The parable was closed out by saying, "And they began to be merry."

Then the words to the old song "Amazing Grace" will have new meaning, which goes like this: "Amazing grace how sweet the sound, that saves a wretch like me, I once was lost, but now I'm found, was blind but now I see." Glory to God!

Eleven

True Believers Are Pioneers for Future Leaders of Tomorrow

From Frederick Douglas all the way to Dr. Martin Luther King Jr., Black Americans have had some extraordinary pioneers leading us into the civil freedoms we experience in this twenty-first century of America. What kind of leaders will the Lord raise up to lead Black America now? Who will pioneer the unchartered territory of where Blacks are going as we follow God into the destiny He has in store for us in the United States of America?

The Lord God used Moses to bring the children of Israel out of slavery from Egypt. They were to leave Egypt and go to the Promised Land. This Promised Land was to be a place that would have all that the people of Israel would ever need. Unfortunately, Moses himself would never get to enter that land. He would only be allowed by God to see it, but not enter into it. Because of an act of disobedience on Moses' part, God would not allow him to go in. God told him to go up on a mountain called Pisgah to see it, because he would not be allowed to go in. This is what God told him.

Deuteronomy 3:27-28 says, "Get thee up into the top of Pisgah, and lift up thine eyes westward, and northward, and southward, and eastward, and behold it with thine eyes: for thou shalt not go over this

Jordan. But charge Joshua and encourage him, and strengthened him: for he shall go over before this people, and he shall cause them to inherit the land which thou shalt see."

This incident calls to memory a similar incident in more recent times. Dr. Martin Luther King, Jr. had a vision of a mountaintop experience just before his death. The day before his death, during a sermon, he said, "Well, I don't know what will happen now. We've got some difficult days ahead. But it doesn't matter with me now. Because I've been to the mountaintop. And I don't mind. Like anybody, I would like to live a long life. Longevity has its place. But I'm not concerned about that now. I just want to do God's will. And He's allowed me to go to the mountain. And I've looked over. And I've seen the Promised Land. I may not get there with you. But I want you to know tonight that we as a people will get to the Promised Land. And I'm happy tonight. I'm not worried about anything; I'm not fearing any man. Mine eyes have seen the glory of the coming of the Lord."

The word *pioneer*, according to Webster's dictionary, is defined as "A person who is among those who first enter or settle a region, thus opening it for occupation and development by others." A pioneer is someone who leads the way or breaks new ground. This is what is needed in the Black homes and communities all across America; mothers and fathers who are willing to be pioneers, then lead their children through the path by which they came, by the help and grace of Almighty God.

True believers are those who are willing to go the distance with God. Those who do not just live for the Lord when things are going good, but those who are committed to Him because He is God. A true believer is one who will read the Word of God and adjust their thinking and life to coincide with what God says, and obeys it to the best of their ability. A true believer is one who has been to the mountaintop and has been in the valley, and still retains their integrity and testimony that He is the King of kings and the Lord of Lords.

What we have more of are parents doing what everyone else is doing. But what they are doing is being done in a negative way, and its results are leading our future leaders, our children, down a path of destruction. There are examples of men and women in the Bible who did just that; lead their children and grandchildren down a path of destruction. The Scripture speaks of Ahab, son of Omri, who became king over Israel. Ahab was king of Israel, but he was weak minded to his wife and a wicked king over Israel. His wife's name was Jezebel, and she dominated her husband, even though he was king. He was a tool in the hands of his wife.

First Kings 22:52 says:"And he did evil in the sight of the Lord and walked in the way of his father, and in the way of his mother, and in the way Jeroboam, the son of Nebat, who made Israel to sin: For he served Baal and worshiped him, and provoked to anger the Lord God of Israel, according to all that his father had done."

As parents, we have an awesome responsibility to teach our children the right way to live. However, we must first live right ourselves so we will know how to instruct our children and their children in life. By living for the Lord and proving God, then we can say to our children, "This is the way to go, walk in it." We will be able to say that because we will have walked in it and found it to be true and right for ourselves first.

When Moses began to charge Joshua and Israel as to what to do and how to do it to get to the Promised Land, these are the words he spoke to them:"Now therefore hearken, O Israel, unto the statues and unto the judgments, which I teach you, for to do them, that ye may live, and go in and possess the land which the Lord God of your fathers giveth you. You shall not add unto the word which I command you, neither shall ye diminish ought from it, that ye may keep the commandments of the Lord your God which I command you.

"Your eyes have seen what the Lord did because of Baal-peor: for all the men that followed Baal-Peor, the Lord thy God hath destroyed them from among you. But ye that cleave unto the Lord your God are alive every one of you this day. Behold I have taught statues and judgements, even as the Lord my God commanded me, that ye should do so in the land whither ye go to possess it. Keep therefore and do them; for this is your wisdom and your understanding in the sight of the nations, which shall hear all these statues, and say, surely this great nation is a wise and understanding people" (Deuteronomy 4:1,6).

With many other words did Moses charge Israel and Joshua with to follow the ways of Almighty God. He gave them words of wisdom that came from his experiences in living for and following the commandments of the Lord. Not only did he tell them he obeyed, but that it was the way that worked best. He told them that they should adapt to the ways of God when they enter into the land, as they possess it.

When our sons and daughters begin to mature and venture out into life for themselves, they will need someone who has pioneered the way for them. Not to dictate what they should do in life, but to give them principles to live by, and principles that will work regardless of what they do in life. There is something that is crippling young Black men and women today before they ever get started on their own, and that is acquiring credit and not knowing how to handle it.

Credit card companies are reaching out more to young people today than ever before, especially college students who are leaving home for the first time. In many cases they have never established a checking account. Things are rapidly changing today, and therefore, children are getting some experience at handling money. But for the most part, the parents who are teaching them today are parents who had to stumble and struggle because they had to find out on their own how to handle credit and debt.

I am forty-eight years old as I complete this book, and I had no idea of how to handle money when I began to mature and become a young man. I have always made good money on jobs but could never seem to get above struggling. Well, that experience can be used to help guide our children as they prepare to go into their own homes and marriages, because the Lord has taught me how to do it now. There are varied ways that parents can be pioneers for their children. Young Blacks need pioneers to help them along in life. One situation that may be considered a negative is giving children everything they want rather than teaching them the value of working for what they need and want.

Blacks tend to do this because we want our children to have what we did not have the opportunity to have when we were growing up. We have an epidemic today of young Black people who do not appreciate what they have, because parents have tried to give them everything. We tend to forget that the reason why we appreciate things is because we worked for what we have acquired, and we have learned the value of working for them. We need to remember as pioneers to instill the same attributes in our children also. If we do not, we will ultimately spoil them and render them ill-prepared for life.

We need as pioneers to remember to teach our young adults the importance of getting involved in political aspects of our country. The right to vote is a precious right that we have that cost our forefathers and mothers dearly for us to have. I am assured that many young Black men and women are not aware that our Black forefathers died that we might have the right to vote. Think of this for a moment! Why did our forefathers care for this right so much that they were willing to give up their lives for something the average Black today cares so little about? We need to teach our children to register and vote, and vote their conscience and vote on the issues and not on a candidate or a particular party.

We have learned from experience how sex before marriage has affected our lives and has made it very difficult as adults. Why shouldn't we as pioneers guide our children and not allow them to practice sex with our consent! I think it would be safe for me to say that almost everyone wishes they could have waited and gotten married before experiencing sex. The reasons for this are easily recognized in today's time, as well as times ago in the past, but it seems to be more prevalent today. In today's time we deal with pregnancy, venereal disease, abortions, AIDS, children born to illegitimate relationships, child support, and custody battles more today than every before.

Many parents have not gone on to further their education. Just because parents did not further their education is no reason why their children cannot go on to higher education today. After many years, those who did not get the education they could have look back and wished they had done more as they get older. If you have walked those roads where you did not take advantage of opportunities, by all means instruct your children and teach them not to follow in those footsteps. Many parents can support their children emotionally and psychologically to go on in school, if not from a point of experience or intellect.

The single most important aspect of life where we should be pioneers is our life in relationship with God. In many cases we may not be able to show our kids how to be successful financially, educationally, or politically. But if we can show them how to live for God, we can teach them how to be successful with integrity, ethics, and morals. We may not be in a position to leave our children a material inheritance when we pass on, but we can leave them the greatest inheritance that can be given to anyone, and that is a legacy of knowing the Lord. If you can pass that on to your children, you will have prepared them for not just life in this world, but also life with God after they cease to exist in this world, if the Lord tarries in His coming.

We do not have a rich heritage when it comes to spiritual leaders in the Black communities of America. This statement needs to be qualified! As I have alluded to in earlier chapters of this book, our heritage has been deeply rooted in traditional religion and not the things of God. Because of this we have not been able to teach our young adults how to know God personally and adhere to the things we have experienced with Him. We have been instructed in how to serve the church, in the church, but not how to have Him as a part of every aspect of our lives.

I remember I was pastor of an inner city church in Baton Rogue, Louisiana. My wife and I served a people who were so gracious to our family. They gave us a Pastor's Appreciation Service we will never forget. They had a special service and collected enough money together to send us on a two-week vacation to Arizona, the best vacation Theresa and I have ever had in all the years of our marriage. While on the road to Arizona, I believe the Lord spoke to my heart about hosting a woman's conference at the church when we returned.

He spoke to me out of the Word of God in Titus 2:4: "That the aged women likewise, that they be in behavior as becometh holiness, not false accusers, not given to much wine, teachers of good things, that they may teach the young women to be sober, to love their husbands, to love their children, to be discreet, chaste, keepers at home, good, obedient to their own husbands, that the Word of God be not blasphemed." Out of that encounter with God came the "Women Professing Godliness Conference."

I believe the Lord put it in my spirit to have two services a day, one during the morning and the main service at night. He wanted to have elderly women to minister to the younger women in the main services. Then we would have younger pastor's wives to minister in the morning services. We had a mixed congregation composed of Blacks and Whites.

We had five night services and four morning services. My wife and I began to search for help in locating women who fit the description. Immediately, it became apparent to us that we had many younger Black women to choose from for the morning services, so much so we had to pray and seek the Lord about which ones to use. But when it came to finding three elderly Black women (at least sixty years old) to teach and preach in the main services, it became a challenge.

Keep in mind, I am not referring to women who were involved in church in the traditional sense, but women who have had walked in the things of God for some time. Women who had the born-again experience with the baptism of the Holy Spirit with the evidence of speaking in other tongues. We wanted to find at least three Black women and two White women who could minister in the conference.

I am aware there may have been others we may not have been aware of during that time. I was born and raised in Baton Rouge and had been saved for approximately fourteen years at this time. I only knew of one Black woman who somewhat fit the description we were looking for. We had no problems finding White women who fit the description. My wife and I began to search for help in locating these women. My wife called the mother-in-law of a pastor's wife we knew and asked for help. She told my wife and me that there were none whom she knew of above sixty years old. Then she made this statement, "Not only do we not have many Black women in this category, we do not have very many Black men either, if any at all."

Most of our Black spiritual leaders who are above sixty years old were in Black traditional churches with twenty, thirty, forty and some even fifty years of experience. These were leaders who fought the teachings of the experiences in the Word of God, such as being born again, and receiving the gift of the Holy Spirit with the evidence of speaking in tongues, and the gifts of the Spirit. These were churches where traditional teachings were being passed on from generation to generation. My heart began to melt when I discovered this. Then I thought of White ministries where the Lord had moved on ministers' hearts for some thirty, forty, fifty and even sixty years ago.

Then I began to recognize how God was now moving among many young Black preaches who are pastors, evangelist, prophets, teachers, and apostles. These are powerful young men and women who are paving the way for young Black preachers coming along the way. But most of these Black ministers did not have someone to pioneer them through difficult situations, and they have made many mistakes. But making the mistakes and trusting the Lord as they go, they will be there to help show others how to depend on the Lord to make it when they feel like quitting, or if they should fail.

I can remember twenty-three years ago when I came to know the Lord in this born-again experience. What a glorious time we had dancing and praising God with no inhibitions, and for long periods of time. The church I attended was in a storefront location in a small shopping center. Around the corner from the church was a bar within the same shopping center. The front of the church was open glass window, and everyone could see in as they passed by, especially during night services when the lights were on.

When we would began to dance and praise God, the glory would manifest, and partygoers would stray in from the bar. Shoppers would stop with amazement just to see what was going on, and because of the operation and the moving of the Holy Spirit, they would come in. I can remember seeing drunks go down on their knees and repenting and accepting Jesus Christ as their Savior.

Oh, how I long for the moving and operation of the Holy Spirit like that again. Where Christians are not ashamed to worship God and praise Him for His goodness. Where we would loose our self-consciousness and take on God consciousness. The pastor of this church was very young at the time, somewhere around twenty-one, or twenty-two years old. He had been saved just a few years prior to starting this church. Eventually, there was a terrible split and many lives were affected. I believe had there been some older Black leaders with good experience in the things of the Spirit, this incident may have been avoided, or at least they would have known how to handle it afterward.

Incidentally, my wife and I were in this same church at this time and did not know each other at that time. We met after the church split and went on to get married. Thank God we came up in a church like that. It was because of the foundation that the young man of God put in us that helped us make it through the years.

I was attending a service once, and a pastor called me up and gave me what I believe to have been a word of knowledge. He said to me by the Spirit of God that as young Black ministers we did not have older Black leadership to follow. Then he said that God was bringing up young Black men such as myself who would make many mistakes in their effort to follow Him, but that these young Black men would be mighty giants of the faith. These giants of the faith would be able to reach back and help young ministers who are coming up. I was humbled then that the Lord had included me in that word. I am even more humbled today to see it happening in my life and ministry.

In the same sense that God will use men and women in the ministry, He will also use many moms and dads to do the same and bring forth Black leaders in the home and church and in the community like never before. As Black women surrender to God, then to their husbands and families, they will began to teach her children by example and by the Word of God. What has been handed down to her that does not work she will abandon and began to do the will of God at any cost. There will be a great cost for her to pay, but she will know the great benefits of her obedience and will ignore the cost and obey God.

Other Black women who may not surrender to the will of God or their families will no doubt ridicule those women who will. They will continue to forsake the things of God and go after the things of the world. They will continue to be selfish and ill responsible. They will continue to be independent. But for the woman who will abandon the entire negative teachings and follow God, she will begin to produce children of strong moral character who believe strongly in God and in themselves. Young men and women who will not be afraid to seize opportunity and have the Word as their foundation. They will understand family values because Momma and Daddy not only told them about the Lord, but they also lived it before them as an example.

Daddy will exemplify to children what it means to be a dad in the eyes of God. He will love, respect, and cherish his wife before the children, family, friends, and neighbors. He will take responsibility in the home and help his wife instill moral values in their children. He will be there as a strength for his wife. He will protect her and support her morally, physically, and spiritually. He will support her financially so she can do all that needs to be done with the children and the home.

The wife will find it easier to want to be submissive to that kind of leadership. The children will see what God's plan for the home looks like as modeled by their parents. The wife will be loving and supportive. She will take care of her husband and children. The children will begin to see a satisfied wife and mother, which will result in security for the children in the home. The family will grow strong together in the fear of the Lord, and they will attend church together. They will understand the principles of not only receiving, but also giving.

Then as the Spirit of God begins to move within the hearts of these young people, He will began to call them into new areas of ministry, business, government, etc. Pride and dignity will once again return to our people. We will abandon despair and despondency. Hope will once again enter into the hearts and lives of Black people.

This can and will be done only as Black men and Black women repent of their misguiding and come home to God through Jesus Christ the Son of God. The Lord will restore them and make of them what He intended from the beginning. Then they will assume the role of pioneer.

Twelve

Why the Forefront Position?

In the introduction to this book, I wrote verbatim the statement that I believe the Holy Spirit spoke to my heart the morning this revelation of Black America was given to me. I have had some wonderful visitations with God, but that morning on June 1, 1992, will always be remembered as one that was extra special. It left me in profound astonishment at what I believe He spoke to my heart. It also qualified my understanding as to how the Holy Spirit used the Old Testament prophets and New Testament apostles to write the Word of God. The Bible says in 2 Peter 1:20-21: "Knowing this first, that no prophecy of the scripture is of any private interpretation. For the prophecy came not in old time by the will of man, but holy men of God spake as they were moved by the Holy Ghost."

I am in no way suggesting that I am in any way equal to these great men of God who penned the Word as the Holy Spirit moved upon them. I am simply stating that I can better understand how it happened, since having received this information by the Holy Spirit regarding Black America. It all came so clear, so fast, it amazes me how the Holy Spirit was able to do that. In a moment's time I understood almost everything written in this book. Of course it took me much longer to put it all together. Here, once again, is the statement I believe the Holy Spirit spoke to my heart that morning, which inspired the writing of this entire book.

"There is a power so strong among the Black people of this nation that it is the very source in which God will bring about to deliver Black people from despair and despondency.

"This source has been abused and misunderstood, yet within itself lies the potential to regain dignity and self-pride.

"In order for God to do what He will began to do very shortly in America, He will have to awaken this sleeping giant.

"This message is the dawning of that awakening.

"We have been hearing for some time now that God is going to bring the Black man to the forefront in these last days, and He will. But this power that I refer to now is the very power that will springboard Black men into position. Ironically, this power has been neglected and abused by the very product in which it will produce, 'The Black man himself.'"

"This unnoticed power source to Black and White men God will use is the Black woman, The Strength of Black America…."

I have heard for quite a few years now that God would use Black men in the last days perhaps like never before. I have been in services where it was stated by Black leadership that when this time comes, it would be considered "our time." Every time I would hear the term used in this way, I would cringe, because I knew what it was intended to mean. The thought behind the statement was "the White man has had his time, now it is our time now." God is no respecter of any particular person or people and would not use this wonderful happening of using Black men to elevate Black men over anyone while diminishing another people.

I believe Moses gave us some insight as to the special abilities or gifting of the Black man as referred to in earlier chapters. In the book of Numbers, 10:29,32, he went to Hobab to ask him to help them to find their way through the wilderness. Hobab was Moses' brother-in-law, a Black man. Moses said to Hobab that God had given them a land that would provide all they needed. This land was the Promised

Land, and He wanted him to come along with them. Moses said that they would give him whatever he needed. Hobab refused and said he was going back to his people. Then Moses said to him, "Leave us not, I pray thee; forasmuch as thou knowest how we are to encamp in the wilderness, and thou mayest be to us instead of eyes."

The wilderness in the Scriptures has always been a place of refining, a rough place, and a place of suffering. God has used the wilderness to prepare many of his prophets and preachers for preparation for ministry. The Bible says of John the Baptist, while he was in the wilderness, in Luke 3:2: "The Word of the Lord came unto John the son of Zacharias in the wilderness." Of course, John the Baptist was to preach righteousness before Jesus was to come; he was considered a forerunner of Jesus.

So for preparation God used the wilderness to prepare John for his ministry. The Bible says in Matthew 4:1 that Jesus himself went into the wilderness: "Then was Jesus led up of the Spirit into the [wilderness] to be tempted of the devil." Luke 4:13-14 records His return from the wilderness: "And when the devil had ended all the temptation, he departed from him for a season. And Jesus returned in the power of the Spirit into Galilee." This is why and how the Lord wants his men to come through the breaking and pruning process after the wilderness experience: "In the power of the Spirit."

Hobab had the necessary experience to encamp in the wilderness because he had been there many times before. For men of God to be used greatly by God, they must be tested and proven greatly before being used. Great men of God have all struggled at some point in their lives. I personally believe that there is no other way for God to show us what we really are inside unless we go through extremely difficult situations.

God already knows what we are inside, but sometimes we think we are better and more self-sufficient than we really are. So God uses the wilderness experience to prune us, and He does it that way in order for us to know what is really within us so we can come to a greater dependency on Him. There are no shortcuts to avoid the wilderness experience. If you are going to be greatly used by God, you will go through this process by way of the wilderness experience.

Before God allowed Israel to go into the Promised Land, He allowed them to go through the wilderness. This may very well have been the reason that Hobab refused to go, in order that God could prune Israel. Of course, Hobab had no way of knowing what God was doing. An example of this can be found in Deuteronomy 8:2, where it says, "And thou shalt remember all the way which the Lord thy God led thee these forty years in the wilderness, to humble thee, and to prove thee, to know what was in thine heart, whether thou wouldest keep his commandments, or no."

God did not need to know what was in Israel's heart. He already knew, but Israel did not know what was in their heart. Jeremiah 17:9 says, "The heart is deceitful above all things, and desperately wicked: Who can know it?" So the Lord allows people to go through experiences to allow them to know what is actually in their heart, because in all actuality we do not know what is in our hearts. Neither does any man until God allows him to go through certain situations, allowing him to see what was in him all along.

If you really want to know where your commitment really is with the Lord, take a good look at how you handled your most difficult trials. It is usually a good barometer. It is usually at that time that the Lord seems to withdraw Himself from you. Although He never does it, it just seems as if He does. In the book of Isaiah 54:7-8, it says, "For a small moment have I forsaken thee; but with great mercies will I gather thee. In a little wrath I hid my face from thee for a moment; but with everlasting kindness will I have mercy on thee, saith the Lord thy redeemer."

Jesus said, "I will never leave you or forsake you even until the end of time." So we understand that God will never actually leave us, but at times He seems to withdraw your awareness of His presence and make you feel as though you are on your own. The wilderness is where this usually happens. Of course the wilderness was a natural physical place, and it can also be spiritually, mentally, and sometimes psychological.

Moses said to Hobab when he asked him to stay, "Leave us not I pray; forasmuch as thou knowest how we are to encamp in the wilderness, and thou mayest be to us instead of eyes." Because of Hobab's experience in the wilderness, Moses was asking him to help show them how to get through rough places. Israel was a type of the church in its infant stages. It was about to embark upon a journey it knew nothing of, and God wanted to prepare them for their entrance into the land He promised them. This was a brand-new beginning for Israel and the first church.

In the time we're living now, the church is not an infant any longer. It has turned away from God and is in deep trouble at this very moment, and the church is about to enter its greatest hour. It has left God and has gone after the things of the world. God is about to get things in order, and He will use Black men as well as White men, and every other ethic group or nationality.

The forefront position is not a position of dominance. It is one that demands love, humility, sensitivity, awareness, direction, power, and compassion. Suffering has a way of making one humble, sensitive, and compassionate. When the Black man comes to God and learns to walk in the forgiveness of the Lord, He will have the ability to see clearly how to walk with the Lord in mercy and compassion. As long as the Black man is away from God, his mind-set is toward what happened to his ancestors in the past, the abuse, neglect, rejection, injustice, prejudice, etc.

And he would not be able to lead anyone anywhere because he would not be able to see. This is what Moses said to Hobab, "that he would be to them instead of eyes," so the Black man will never be any use in the forefront position if he cannot see. Jesus said it this way in Luke 6:41-42: "And why beholdest thou the mote that is in thy brothers eye, but perceivest not the beam that is in thine own eye? Either how canst thou say to thy brother, Brother, let me pull out the mote that is in thine eye, when thou thyself beholdest not the beam that is in thine own eye?" Amazing grace, I was blind but now I see!

The Black man will be in no condition to lead if he does not get himself right with God. We have Black leaders today who speak very boldly regarding Black issues of injustice and racism. They are not as effective as they could be because they themselves are showing the racism and unforgiveness in their own hearts.

I believe Dr. Martin Luther King Jr. was very effective in his efforts because he had a personal relationship with God. He learned to walk in forgiveness, and it showed in his personal life as well as his public life. He spoke with convictions. He said some very strong things that were factual and true, but he said those things with much compassion. He was trying to bring a people together. It seems as though Black leaders today are trying to divide rather than unify and strengthen.

There are leaders who have been tempered through adversity, who understand what it means to be misunderstood, who understand what it means to be discriminated against, who know what it is to suffer, to be less fortunate, and yet they still operate from a heart of understanding, compassion, forgiveness, and love. It was said of Jesus in the book of Isaiah 53:3: "He was despised and rejected of men; a man of sorrows, and acquainted with grief: and we hid as it were our faces from him; he was despised, and we esteemed him not." Jesus was a man who understood the hurts and pains of all men because He had experienced them Himself. One who leads must have acquaintance with the problems and experiences of those he is to lead.

In the book of Hebrews 2:17, it says, "Wherefore in all things it behoved him to be made like unto his brethren" [flesh and blood] "that he might be a merciful and faithful high priest in things pertaining to God, to make reconciliation for the sins of the people." In Hebrews 4:14-15, it says, "Seeing then that we have a great high priest, that is passed into the heavens, Jesus the Son of God, let us hold fast our profession. For we have not an high priest which cannot be touched with the feeling of our infirmities; but was in all points tempted like as we are, yet without sin." So Jesus Himself went through much suffering and affliction, so that he could understand what those whom He came to minister to were going through daily in life.

The church is entering into its final stage before the coming of the Lord in the Rapture. God is about to bring in a harvest of souls all over the world. God is looking for leaders who will be able to identify with those in all walks of life, who have been touched with their pain and suffering and will be willing to love and minister to them as they are.

In Black homes all across America, God is calling Black men to the forefront in their homes. Somehow the male role model has vanished or has been subverted into a role model that has become weak and feminine rather than masculine and subservient. Black women in

Black communities need strong Black men in their lives who are not afraid to love and are compassionate and supportive.

Men of responsibility, integrity, and commitment. Men who will mentor their children and, especially, their sons with time, energy, and love. Men who will nurture and support their daughters to become secure within themselves, so they can have the love of a man in their life to help complete them at home. And they will not feel the need to search for the kind of love that can only come from a father.

The forefront position in the church will be experiencing a changing of the guards. The forefront position in Black homes has been vacant for too long a period of time. But thank God He is about to do a new thing. God says it this way in Isaiah 43:19: "Remember ye not the former things, neither consider the things of old. Behold, I will do a new thing; now it shall spring forth; shall ye not know it? I will even make a way in the wilderness, and rivers in the desert." Malachai 4:6 says, "And he shall turn the heart of fathers to the children, and the heart of the children to their fathers, lest I come and smite the earth with a curse."

Without Black women in correct position with God and in their homes, strong Black leaders will never come to the forefront as they should. My sisters in the Lord, God the Holy Ghost is waiting for the woman to say, "Here am I, Lord, use me!" Will you be one He can use?

About the Author

I was born and raised in Baton Rouge, Louisiana. I was born into a wonderful family of four sisters and two brothers: Gloria, Beatrice, Ruby, and Barbara (we lost Ruby to Cancer). My two brothers were, Leonard and Rivers. I am the youngest of all seven. My mother, bless her heart, I felt did a tremendous job in raising seven children alone. She was one tough lady but as sweet as they come. They just don't make them like that anymore. Her name is Iola M. Brown, better known by everyone as "Ma Dea."

All of my family was athletic in some way. We used to have outings when all the family would play softball. Ma Dea would be right out there with us, and she had game too. Both of my brothers were captains on our high school baseball team at Capital High School. For me, growing up under that much athletic talent, playing baseball came natural for me.

I started playing organized ball from the time I was five years old, until I was twenty-four or twenty-five years old. I followed in my brother's footsteps in becoming the captain of Capital High School's baseball team. I went to college on an athletic scholarship in baseball. My entire life was centered on baseball. I was a clean-cut young man and took the game quite seriously. My mother would follow our team wherever we would play, winning season or not she was there.

As I began life on the college campus, things began to change for the worse. I began experimenting with drugs and entered into a life-style that took me away from all that I loved. I eventually walked out of school and started down a path that took me downward. I began to gamble on pool tables just to make money. My game had gotten so good, I had to leave Baton Rouge to play because I had gotten too good. While on my way to New Orleans, almost twenty-four years ago, I had a visitation from the Lord. I liken it unto the experience the apostle Paul had on his way to Damascus.

I drove a little yellow Volkswagen Beetle then, and the presence of the Lord entered that car. I did not know what was happening to me at the time, but I came to recognize it was his presence. He so changed my life that when I returned home, it was difficult for people to understand what had happened to me. You see, the life-style I was living was nothing like the experience I had. As I would try to explain to everyone what happened to me, I would began to cry, and everyone thought something was wrong with me. They thought I had gotten a hold of some kind of drugs that affected me mentally.

I had some things in the car with me that was against the law. I had cigarettes in my pocket, and God's presence was overwhelming. I cried out in repentance to Him, and somewhere I got strength to throw everything I had in the car that was wrong out onto Interstate 10 eastbound. I later learned that strength came from him as he was with me when I cried out. I found something that was greater than anything I ever knew, and I did not need all the other stuff anymore.

I began to grow in the Lord and read his Word daily. I remember when I would begin praying I would pray so loud I felt I would disturb my mother, we lived in a small three-room house. I had moved back home after making a mess of my life, I was divorced and lost jobs, etc. My desire to pray increased, so I had to find somewhere to pray for extended periods. The church my family attended was a few blocks from the house, so I would go there at night to pray.

The lady who cleaned the church lived right next door to it; her name was Mrs. Clara Richardson. She would open the door to allow me to go in at nighttime and pray when no one else was there. One night, as I was praying, the Spirit of God visited with me. Something that was strange to me happened; I later found out it was called being slain in the Spirit. His presence so overcame me, I went out, and went down on the floor out in the Spirit. While I was out, I heard the Lord ask me if I would preach His gospel. Of course I said yes I would without hesitation! I thought I was ready to preach for him right away, but that came much later on, I did not realize that there would be training and preparation involved.

Since that time I have been pastor of three churches, I have preached as an Evangelist, I have been on the Pastoral staff at Jimmy Swaggart Ministries in Baton Rouge, and I have worked on the staff with Promise Keepers out of Denver Colorado. I continue to preach today as an evangelist. My life has been so wonderful since meeting Jesus Christ as my Lord and Savior.

The Lord blessed me with a wonderful wife, Sis. Theresa R. Brown, who in her own right is a dynamic preacher and minister, she has preached in women's conferences, and lead women's meetings in the churches we had as pastor. We have been married for twenty years, the best twenty years of my life.

I thank God for coming into my life and saving me as he did. I do not know where I would be if He had not come into my life when He did. If anything I may have said in this book blesses anyone, all of the credit for it goes to the Lord. For I was nothing when He found me, but He has made me His, and I thank God He did.

The Strength of Black America
Order Form

Postal orders: P.O. 77976
Baton Rouge, LA 70879

Telephone orders: 225-296-5546

E-mail orders: cbministries@aol.com

Please send *The Strength of Black America* **to:**

Name: _____

Address: _____

City: _____ State: _____

Zip: _____

Telephone: (_____) _____

Book Price: $13.00

Shipping: $3.00 for the first book and $1.00 for each additional book to
cover shipping and handling within US, Canada, and Mexico.
International orders add $6.00 for the first book and $2.00 for
each additional book.

Or order from:
ACW Press
5501 N. 7th. Ave. #502
Phoenix, AZ 85013

(800) 931-BOOK

or contact your local bookstore